Blackhole in the Dust:
The Novels of Toni Morrison

Blackhole in the Dust:
The Novels of Toni Morrison

Kavita Arya

ADHYAYAN

ADHYAYAN PUBLISHERS & DISTRIBUTORS
New Delhi-110002

Published by
ADHYAYAN PUBLISHERS & DISTRIBUTORS
4378/4B, 105, J.M.D. House, Murari Lal Street
Ansari Road Darya Ganj, New Delhi - 110002
Ph.: 011-23263018, 011-23277156, Fax: 23280028
Email: adhyayanpublishers@yahoo.com

Blackhole in the Dust: The Novels of Toni Morrison

Edition 2010
ISBN 978-81-8435-220-7

Printed in India

Published by Harish Chandra Yadav for Adhyayan Publishers & Distributors, Delhi. Laser Typesetting at V. M. Graphics and Printed at Tarun Offset Printers, Delhi

Dedicated to
my Maa
who have enlightened and blessed me
in every sphere of my life

Acknowledgements

When years of earnest research finally translate into a book, it is very easy to take all the credit and pat oneself on the back for this accomplished work. The truth remains, however, that no work of such magnitude can be achieved without a whole network of support system. I consider myself both fortunate and blessed to have been associated with people who were very helpful. Although words alone are not adequate, they are all I have to acknowledge to express my deep gratitude to all the people who helped me during the research work.

I feel great pleasure in expressing my gratitude to my supervisor, Dr. Sanjay Kumar, who consistently supported and guided me in my research work.

I wish to acknowledge my gratitude to Prof. Sacchidanand Mohanty, Osmania University, Hyderabad, for his encouragement during the writing of this book.

My special thanks goes to Prof. R.S. Sharma and Prof. J.B. Mishra for giving their guidance and support.

I am thankful to Prof. A.K. Tripathy, Prof. R.K. Shukla, Prof. V. Tripathi, and all the teachers of our English Department.

A very warm thanks goes to the staff of the I.A.C.I.S. at Hyderabad, A.I.R.C. at Mumbai and S.R. Gayakwad Library, Banaras Hindu University where I had access to many priceless resources.

I wish to thank from the bottom of my heart to Jay

Govind Mishra, for giving me constant encouragement and showing great optimism and faith in my abilities.

I owe a special debt to Dr. Purnima Srivastava for her support and encouragement. I would like to give my special thanks to my friends who helped me in unique and extraordinary ways. The solace and assurance they gave whenever I seemed to lose sight of the goal will remain with me forever. The progress and good wishes they constantly sent my way will always have a special place in my heart.

Finally and most importantly, I want to express my deep gratitude to my mother Mrs. Mamta Devi, my brothers, and relatives, all of whom stood firmly by me during the most difficult moments and never allowed me to give up. This accomplishment would not have been possible without the cooperation and support of my husband Rishiraj Gupta. Although much has been said, there is still more that remains unsaid because debts of this magnitude are impossible to repay. All I can say is that the important part of this achievement belongs also to each person mentioned in these pages. Finally, this success is theirs as much as it is mine.

Kavita Arya

Foreword

A Book on Toni Morrison is a proud privilege of the writer Dr. Kavita Arya. Toni Morrison, a black American writer is the recipient of Nobel Prize for literature in 1993 and a winner of Pulitzer Prize in 1988 for her fiction beloved. Racial violence, issues of sexism and classism have been dominant in American society and to leaving them to the fore front of the modern world had been the aim of this great author. The writer has picturised her inner conscious through the study of her writings.

Whereas Toni Morrison faced all problems of racism, slavery, discrimination between males & female writers, differentiation between black and white authors, with boldness, courage and literary expression, Dr. Kavita Arya, in her work has very prominently brought forward the inner mind, thoughts and expressionism of Toni Morrison.

Deep studies, which touch the inner feelings of a person, are rare, as author Dr. Arya deserves all appreciation for this useful work, which she has so clearly and frankly described in this book.

I congratulate the Dr. Kavita Arya on her fruitful work and wish that all those concerned with racism, sexism, colonialism, gender discrimination, black and white slavish attitude, should read this piece of excellent work.

Chitralekha Singh

Preface

Being Black and female gives a unique perspective to Toni Morrison in her writings. From her first novel, *The Bluest Eye,* to the latest, *Paradise,* we come across the deleterious nexus of racism, sexism and classism. Our effort has been to uncover and analyze this nexus and how this nexus critically affects the lives of Black women characters in her novels. The agony and distress of the Black women is perhaps the strongest theme of her fiction. The crux of our approach is to unveil the damaging effect of dominant standard of beauty on her characters, which makes them aberrant and eccentric. In the course of her literary career as an author, Morrison has become an African-American woman writer to reckon with. She has been amply recognized for her combined greatness as a voice for black people and as a master craftsperson of the dominant literary artistic form.

Morrison belongs to the group of African-American women writers – Maya Angelou, Toni Cade Bambara, Paul Marshall, Alice Walker, and Gloria Naylor – for whom writing is a liberating tool, a subversive strategy and an artistic mode for self-expression. Combining the aims of the Black Freedom Movement and Women's Liberation, Morrison seeks to produce literature, which is irrevocably and indisputably black.

The book is divided into nine chapters. The first chapter forms the introduction and deals with the history of African-

American people especially women. Societal and psychological restrictions have critically affected the lives of African-American women. They have undergone a different kind of a social reality from the Whites, which consequently make them conscious of the most pressing problem, which is evident in their movement as well as in their writings. Before the awakening of Black feminist consciousness, African-American women were projected as stereotypes in the canon of American literature. Neither White writers nor Black male writers were able to project the image of African-American women from the insider's point of view. Even earlier Black women writers also talk about only racial subjugation or write in order to get an appreciation from White audience. So the chapter also shows how the Black feminist movement emerges and talks about the history of African-American women writers. It also seeks to place Morrison in the literary tradition of Black women's writing. Her novels focus on the realities of racial, sexual and capitalistic discrimination within the American context.

The second chapter of the book is concerned with Morrison's first novel, *The Bluest Eye* (1970). It is about the difficulty of achieving individuality and full humanity in an objectifying and manipulating society. In *The Bluest Eye* the protagonist Pecola, an eleven-year-old Black girl, suffers from the lack of self-esteem because she does not have white skin, blonde hair and blue eyes. Here Morrison investigates how the standard of European White beauty has deleterious effects on the psychology of a Black female adolescent. This dominant culture has maimed her so much that she goes mad. Though racial violence is dominant in the entire novel, the issues of sexism and classism are also present in the fabric of novel. The novel also shows that the migration of Blacks from the despotic South to the North and to the central Mid-West gives rise to various problems relating to race, gender and class and also involves a loss of identity for them as human beings.

The third chapter deals with Morrison's second novel *Sula* (1973) where the thrust is on the possibility of freedom and the individuality of African-American women. Sula, the protagonist, is an iconoclast. She is a "living criticism of the dreadful lives of resignation other women live." As a young girl, she startles the community with her extreme emotional impulses and grows into a "strange, strong, and independent woman." She rejects "behavioural standards of all kinds" and attempts to "rely solely on herself." Even though the focus of the novel is on gender bias, the racial issues – the origin of the Bottom with its roots in slavery and the lack of development of Deweys – are interwoven into the fabric of the novel. The concept of gender with its interconnection to race and class forms an indispensable part of the novel. Morrison delves deep into the issue of a person's rights and identity in terms of gender. Thus in *Sula,* Morrison's focus shifts to the African-American woman as an individual, struggling towards freedom and selfhood. Sula hates the traditional norms of feminine respectability like family, marriage, children, parental care, sexual mores and the concept of steady job. She hates to see a woman only as a wife, mother, and daughter. In *Sula* Morrison attempts to show the individuality of an African-American woman, struggling for emancipation and identity. The exploitation of African-American women in America, especially in the first quarter of the twentieth century, is documented in the novel.

The fourth chapter is devoted to a study of *Song of Solomon* (1977) in which class, in relation to race and gender, becomes more of a focal point. In this novel Morrison deals with the themes of initiation and quest for family roots, which, in turn, are linked to the search for Afro-American cultural heritage. The protagonist of *Song of Solomon,* unlike her earlier novels, is a Black male, Milkman Dead. Morrison's focus in the third novel becomes more externally directed, moving beyond the intimacy of the enclosed communities found in her first two novels. *Song of Solomon* gives an interesting example of the manner in which equations of power and the levels of class, gender and race operate in a literary work. This novel is written from a male vantage point. Still, gender oppression of the female emerges as an issue of prominence as in her previous novels with the exception that the focus of attention is more on the middle-class Black women.

Song of Solomon shows the effects of middle-class values on African-American families. Like Alex Haley's *Roots*, it illustrates the importance of African awareness and acceptance of their history in order to liberate themselves from race and class oppression. Though Milkman's quest for his identity is the dominant thread of the novel, the major obstacle he has to overcome is the deadening effect of capitalism. Milkman is accidentally propelled into a search for his self as a result of his desire for gold. The long journey leads him back through his personal past to a racial history. His knowledge liberates him, and he begins to respect the poor blacks around him as well as the Sweet women, Pilate and Hagar, who have continuously helped him. *Song of Solomon*, thus, marks a qualitative leap over her previous novels.

The fifth chapter deals with *Tar Baby* (1981). *Tar Baby* gives voice to much that is left unspoken in the previous novels. Unlike her earlier novels, in *Tar Baby*, she places the issues of race, gender and class in a contemporary context and does not associate them with an earlier time and place. *Tar Baby* exposes all the conflicts that result from the cultural encounter between the colonizers and colonized. The two protagonists in *Tar Baby*, Son and Jadine, are sharply divided in their attitudes to the dominant ruling class as well as to their own traditional culture. They must struggle together to resolve their own class interests in order to unite.

The sixth chapter is about Toni Morrison's masterpiece *Beloved* (1987), a novel about slavery and about the history of oppression founded on race. This not only unveils that "peculiar phase of slavery" which "has generally been kept veiled," i.e., the tale of sexual abuse but also critically comments on the inequities that Black women still face. Indeed, all of Morrison's novels have been constructed and are magically unsettled by the unique character of historical memory for African-Americans. With each of her earlier novels, Morrison was inching her way back beyond the twentieth-century experience of racism, poverty and injustice towards its origins in the history of slavery. Based on the most oppressed period of slavery in the history of African people, *Beloved* dramatizes a haunting amalgam of the past and present experiences of an escaped female Sethe, tracing the heroine's quest for meaning and wholeness in slavery and in freedom. Through flashbacks to past tragedies and deeply symbolic delineations of continued emotional and psychological suffering, the novel explores the hardships endured by Sethe and her family during the Reconstruction era. It is Morrison's goal in this work to demonstrate that collectivism is the first step in eradicating the racial oppression and class exploitation of African people.

The seventh chapter deals with Toni Morrison's *Jazz* (1992). It adds a new dimension to the remedy for the African dilemma. Just as African people as a whole must bond together to survive and to progress, so also must African women—the most exploited adult sector in the African community—help one another in order to live healthy and wholesome lives. Morrison's purpose in the novel is to make fiction do what music does whereby she exploits the mode of jazz to depict the experience of the Black community during the 1920s known as the Jazz Age. Just as the musical mode of jazz is known to have used familiar material to express various sentiments, using performer and audience, the fictional mode of jazz, used in the novel, establishes quick contact between the characters and the reader. The novel traces the path to the understanding of self, Violet, a wronged women, comes to in her relationships with other black women—Dorcas, Alice, and Felice. Though it starts with Violet's inability to understand Dorcas, she finally does achieve this understanding through her interaction with Dorcas' aunt Alice and her friend, Felice. Defining themselves through bonding on various levels—physical, intellectual, emotional and psychic—with other black women, these black women seek their own identity.

The eighth chapter of the book deals with Morrison's

latest novel *Paradise* (1997). It is her first novel after winning the Nobel prize for literature. It is the third in the series of her novels exploring themes from African-American history. *Beloved* is about slavery; *Jazz* deals with urban life in the Jazz era; and *Paradise* is set in contemporary times. It is inspired by stories of the all-Black communities established after slavery came to an end. *Paradise* is another work in which African-American women of various ages and various backgrounds find freedom and happiness in isolation from a racial and sexually oppressive society in a convent in Oklahoma far away from everywhere. But, unfortunately, their 'paradise' is short lived. The dominant, patriarchal society of Ruby does not allow for a 'Herland' to exist, because this Herland threatens its basic power structure and questions its dominance. Hence, it is out to extinguish this 'paradise' before the concept of this kind of freedom contaminates its hegemony.

The last chapter of the book shows how an evolutionary pattern emerges in Toni Morrison's novel. The nexus among race, gender and class is the cause of oppression of Black women in White America. Each of her novels emphasizes a different but connected facet of the oppression of the Blacks. Morrison's treatment of the problem shows that she is not merely an accomplished writer but a very conscious artist too.

Contents

Introduction

A celebrated African-American author, Toni Morrison was born as Chloe Anthony Wofford on 18 February 1931 in Lorain, Ohio. Her parents George Wofford and Ramah Willis Wofford's positive self-image influenced her profoundly. She received her B.A. degree in English literature from Howard University in 1953 and a Masters degree from Cornell University in 1955 where she worked on the theme of suicide in William Faulkner and Virginia Woolf. In 1958 she married a Jamaican architect Harold Morrison and had two sons, Harold Fo d (1962) and Slade Kevin (1966). She was divorced in 1964, and thereafter she began her literary career. Her debut novel, *The Bluest Eye,* (1970), *Sula* (1973), *Song of Solomon* (1977), *Tar Baby* (1981), *Beloved* (1987), *Jazz* (1992), and her creative output continued with the publication of her latest fiction *Paradise* (1997).

Apart from fiction she has written several essays: "What the Black Woman Thinks about Women's Lib" (1971), "Behind the Making of the Black Book" (1974), "City Limits, Village Values: Concepts of the Neighbourhood in Black Fiction" (1981), "Recitatif" (1983), "Rootedness: The Ancestors as Foundation" (1984), "Memory Creation and Writing" (1984), "A Knowing So Deep" (1985), "The Site of Memory" (1987), "Unspeakable things Unspoken" (1989), a volume of literary criticism, *Playing in the Dark: Whiteness and the Literary Imagination* (1992), and a collection of essays which include "Racing Justice," "En-gendering Power," essays on Anita Hill, Clarence Thomas and "The Contribution of Social Reality" (1993).

Morrison has written a play as well, *Dreaming Emmett* (1986), which is based on the life of Emmett Till, a young boy, who was lynched by a mob in Mississippi in 1954. Her writings have won both critical and popular acclaim, and she has won several national and international awards. In 1977 she received the "National Book Critics Circle Award" and the "American Academy and Institute of Arts and Letters Award" for *Song of Solomon.* In 1981 she appeared on the cover of *Newsweek.* She was the first African-American woman to be featured on the cover of a national magazine after Zora Neale Hurston in 1943. *Tar Baby* was on the best seller list for four months. In 1988 she was awarded the "Pulitzer Prize" and the "Robert F. Kennedy Award" for *Beloved.* In 1992 *Jazz* and *Playing in the Dark: Whiteness and the Literary Imagination* both were on the best seller list for four months. And on 7 October, 1993, the Swedish Academy awarded Morrison the "Nobel Prize" for literature. She became the first African-American woman to win this award.

Morrison is a versatile genius who also has had a diverse career as a teacher, editor and writer. She began her career as a teacher first at Texas Southern University, Houston, from 1955 to 1957 and then at Howard University as an instructor from 1957 to 1964. In 1965, she became an editor at Random House. After ten years she resumed her teaching career as a visiting professor at Yale University between 1976 and 1978, and then from 1984 to 1989 as the Albert Schweitzer Professor of the Humanities at the State University of New York at Albany. In 1989 she became Robert F. Goheen Professor of the Humanities at Princeton University.

She never intended to be a writer. She turned to fiction to relieve her loneliness:

> I never planned to be a writer. I was in a place where there was nobody I could talk to and have a real

> conversation with. And I think I was also very unhappy. So I wrote then for that reason. And then, after I had published, it was sort of a compulsive thing because it was a way of knowing, a way of thinking that I found really necessary. (qtd. in Jane Bakerman, p. 30)

Before we examine the works of Morrison, it is useful to know the history of African-Americans in the U.S.A. As Melvin Drimmer suggests,

> "Amerika, du hast es besser," wrote the aged Goethe, and Americans have agreed. America was created as a paradise, a garden supposedly free of the problems that afflicted the old world. Yet we have been unable to reconcile America's original sin, Negro racism, with the image of the paradise. (Drimmer, p. 75)

When we glance through the history of America we find it full of barbarism, violence and bloodshed against African-Americans. It is generally agreed that for the first time a large number of Blacks were brought to Jamestown, Virginia, in 1619. And since then the history of enslavement began. The Whites created complicated cultural and legal system in order to justify discrimination against the African-Americans. According to them African-Americans were "without souls, a strange exotic new kind of creature" (Ranveer, p. 2). Maltreatment and persecution of African-Americans by Whites show as if they belonged to a different species and were less than human: "The status of the Negro was that of servants" (Drimmer, p. 79).

The racial inferiority of the African-Americans and hence the discriminatory practices against them were supposedly proved through various ethnological studies. As Barabara Christian explains,

> The characteristics of Blacks' racial inferiority, which Jefferson had so impressionistically discussed in the 1790s, were, by the 1830s, buttressed by scientific argument. Ethnological writers such as Richard Colfax,

> Samuel Cartwright and Josiah Nott detailed the physical deficiencies of the Negro, his cranial characteristics, his facial angles, and concluded that intellectually the Negro was incapable of being the equal of Whites. Their utterances quickly became a racist ideology in the United States. This school of thought also had polygamist tendencies, however that is, many ethnological writers believed the different races of men had different origins and that God created many pairs of the human race. ("Shadows Uplifted", p. 186)

The condition of African-American women was more grim and serious since they were not only Black but also female and poor. They were triply enslaved in a racist, patriarchal and classist society. Their destiny was to suffer in silence. They were compelled to occupy the most marginal position in the American society. Hence this promised land became a "great prison" and an "octopus of exploitation" for them (Ranveer, p. 1).

According to Calvin Hernton,

> [F]rom time to time in America various individuals and groups besides Negroes have been victims of prejudice, discrimination, injustice, persecution and outright murder.... But it has been the Negro woman, more than anyone else, who has borne the constant agonies of racial barbarity in America from the very first day. She was brought in chains to the soil. The Negro woman through the years has suffered (and endured) every sexual outrage (with all of the psychological ramifications) that a democratic society can possibly inflict upon a human being. The sexual atrocities that the Negro woman has suffered in the United States, South and North, and what these atrocities have done to her personality as a female character, is a tale more bloody and brutal than most of us can imagine. (p. 123)

After their arrival on this alien soil, African-American women had to endure the worst kind of exploitation. As women they had to satisfy their master's lust. They were treated as sexpots and puppets in the hands of their White masters. They were not allowed to raise their voice against this atrocity. Those who did try to oppose were cruelly beaten, lynched and burnt alive. Their owners branded with hot irons the letters of their names on their cheeks and cropped a piece of each to claim their ownership. "Some masters branded the letters of their names on inside of both their legs" (Katz, p. 87) to assert that the slave women and their private parts belonged to them only.

Female slaves were defined in terms of their breeding capacity. The White man treated them less as humans and more like chattels. Their bodies were used and exploited for procreating more and more slaves. Slave owners saw each new child as a means of improving their economic condition. Drimmer gives a very vivid account of it:

> She [a girl about twenty years of age] . . . is very prolific in her generating qualities, and affords a rare opportunity for any person who wishes to raise a family of strong, healthy servants for . . [his] own use. . . . (p. 75)

So their reproductive ability becomes problematic for them. The rapaciousness of the Whites forced African-American women to do both a man's and woman's work. Not only were they forced to breed, but they were also given very little time and facility to regain their health. They had to come back to work only after two weeks of childbirth. Their children were brought to the field with them, and they were given breaks during the day to nurse their children.

African-American women always lived under the fear that one day their children would be taken away from them and sold. Moses Grandy gives an eyewitness account of the treatment of the African-American women by the overseer:

> On the estate I am speaking of those women who had sucking children suffered much from their breasts

> becoming full of milk, the infants being left at home; they therefore could not keep up with the other hands. I have seen the overseer beat them with rawhide, so that the blood and milk flew mingled from their breasts. A woman who gives offence in the field, and is large in the family way, is compelled to lie down over a hole made to receive her corpulency, and is flogged with the whip, or beat with a paddle, which had holes in it; at every stroke comes a blister. One of my sisters was so severely punished in this way, that labour was brought on, and the child was born in the field. This very overseer, Mr. Brooks, killed in this manner a girl named Mary: her father and mother were in the field at the time. (p. 168)

Whites forced African-American women to be servants of their women and wet nurses for their children while their own children were neglected. Not only White but African-American men also discarded them, so they were "black among the blacks" and "slave of the slaves".

During slavery African-American women were supposed to nurture their families and protect their family members in the absence of their husbands, a responsibility which they managed very well. As they had to be tough and strong in order to look after their families, African-American men began to think of them as masculinized, castrating, domineering and unfeminine.

The abolition of slavery by law mitigated their agony to some extent. However, it could not eradicate all their pain and suffering. Even after the abolition of slavery, they continued to be ill-treated by the Whites. African-American men became sharecroppers, and African-American women were taken as housemaids of the Whites. White men were still free to have sex with them whenever they wanted. They characterized African-American women as "loose" women who tried to seduce them. In 1874, an African-American congressman announced, "we want more protection from the

Whites invading our houses and destroying the virtue of our women than they from us" (qtd. in Ranveer, pp. 4-5).

After the abolition of slavery, miscegenation became the biggest threat to the Whites. As a result laws and taboos were sanctioned to prevent the intermingling of race:

> As a means of protecting Whites from the taint of Black blood, some states as early as 1680 banned interracial marriages. By the early 1700s Blacks had becomes associated in the American mind with the ape, especially the orang-utan (qtd. in "Shadows Uplifted", p. 183).

> They labelled Blacks as "lewd, lascivious and wanton" ("Shadows Uplifted", p. 183).

Just as White men were protective of their women, African-American men also sought ways of making their women unapproachable for White men. Both African-American and White men warned their women against having inter-racial relationship because they would lead to the exploitation and degradation of their womanhood. On the one hand, African-American men advocated the imposition of such restrictions on their women; on the other hand, they did not consider it wrong to have a relationship with White women themselves.

African-American men started to emulate the norms of White men. They began to internalize the norms and standards of White men. As a result they themselves joined hands with their victimizers and started to despise their own women. Hence African-American women became desperate to prove their value as human beings:

> [T]hat man over there says women need to be helped into carriages, and lifted over ditches, and to have the best place everywhere. Nobody ever helps me into carriage, or over mud puddle, or gives me any best place! And ain't I a woman? Look at me! Look at my arms! I have ploughed, and planted, and gathered into barns, and no man could head me!

> And ain't I a woman? I would work and eat as much as a man – when I could get it – and bear the lash as well! And ain't I a woman? I have borne thirteen children and seen them most of all sold off to slavery, and when I cried out with my mother's grief, none but Jesus heard me! And ain't I a woman? (qtd. in Loewenberg and Bogin, p. 235)

In fact, to be a woman, Black or White, is a bane and curse. Man is always characterized by greater strength and activity than a woman. When we turn the pages of history, it tells the story of the ill-treatment, humiliation and subjugation of women. Sarah Grimke observes,

> Man has subjugated woman to his will, used her as a means to promote his selfish gratification to minister to his sensual pleasure, to be instrumental in promoting his comfort; but never has he desired to elevate her to that rank she was created to fill: He has done all he could do to debase and enslave her mind. . . . (qtd. in Bhatnagar, p. 48).

After a long time a momentous awakening came in the latter half of the nineteenth century, when women started to protest against patriarchal hegemony and male domination. Feminism broadly refers to this movement, which fights for the parity of all women with men. The term was first used by the French dramatist, Alexander Dumas, in 1872 in a pamphlet "L'Hommefemme." It is also called Aphraism after Aphra Behn, a seventeenth-century feminist and political activist. Feminism protests against the prevalent disparities and inequities and strives to break from the stultifying male ideology. It struggles for economic, social and gender equalities. The eminent writers who inaugurated this movement through their writings in the late eighteenth and nineteenth century are Mary Wollstoncraft's *A Vindication of the Rights of Woman* (1792), John Stuart Mill's "The Subjugation of Women" (1869) and Margaret Fuller's "Woman in the Nineteenth Century" (1845). They set-off a new wave of feminism.

Virginia Woolf has been an eminent voice in feminist criticism. Her famous *A Room of One's Own* (1929) and many other writings argue for the abolition of all gender inequities. She realizes that patriarchal society is the root cause of women's oppression. She believes that women have always confronted social and economic shackles in their literary ambitions. She herself was acutely conscious of the discrimination practised against women in education. She was taught no Greek, for instance. She believed that when women finally achieve social and financial parity with men, there would be nothing to stop them from freely developing their artistic talents. After Virginia Woolf a new frankness about sexuality (adultery, lesbianism, etc.) enters into women's writing. From the early a more angry tone emerges in the writings of Penelope Mortiner, Muriel Spark and Doris Lessing.

French feminist Simone de Beauvoir claims that "femininity is manufactured in society". She observes,

> Humanity is male and man defines woman not in herself but in relation to him, she is not regarded as an autonomous being. . . . For him she is sex – absolute sex, no less. She is defined and differentiated with reference to man and not he with reference to her; she is the incidental, the inessential as opposed to the essential. He is the subject, he is the Absolute. She is the other. (p. 16)

She argues that women have been made marginal, and the maltreatment has been compounded by men's belief that women are less than men by nature. She claims that "one is not a woman; one becomes one".

According to Raman Seldon, there are five main areas in which woman under a patriarchal value system is considered inferior to man but under a feminist value system, she has been shown as the stronger of the two. They are (1) biology, (2) experience, (3) discourse, (4) the unconscious, and (5) social and economic conditions. Due to her biological function she has been played down by men and treated as the "other." The saying "tota mulier in uterno" (women is nothing but a womb) sums up this attitude. Biologically a woman's body has always been considered inferior to that of man. Men need not depend upon another body for the untying of the so-called "Gordian Knot of Nature". But some radical feminists refuse to accept it and claim that her biological attributes are superior to those of men because she has certain life experiences such as ovulation, menstruation and parturition. Further a woman's experience is different. Like man, she seeks things but has different perceptions, ideas, outlook and feelings. Since she has a unique biological function, her mode of thinking is also different from that of a man.

Dale Spender's *Man-Made Language* considers that women have been oppressed by a male-dominated language. For instance there is the use of "man" or "mankind" for human beings in general, "Chairman" and Spokesman" for both the sexes, and the pronouns "he" and "his" to indicate neuter gender nouns such as "God", "human being", "child", "inventor", "author", "policeman" etc. Language reflects the deep-rooted attitudes enshrined in our minds; the male is the norm in the world of language and, therefore, in the outside world. According to Robinlakoff, male utterance is "stronger", so it must be adopted by women if they wish to achieve social equality with men. Radical feminists think that women have been brainwashed by this type of ideology, which produces stereotypes of strong men and vulnerable women.

The psychoanalyst theorists, Lacan and Kristeva, have discovered a fourth focus, the process of the unconscious. Some feminist authors have broken completely with biologism by associating the female with these processes, which tend to undermine the authority of man's discourse. Whatever encourages or initiates a free play of meanings and prevents closure is regarded as female. Female sexuality is revolutionary, subversive, heterogeneous, and open. This approach is less likely to run the risks of ghettoization and stereotyping, since it denies defining female sexuality; if there is a female principle, it is simply to remain outside the male definition of the female.

Virginia Woolf was the first female critic to add a sociological dimension (5th focus) in her analysis of women's writing. Since then, Marxist feminists have sought to alter social and economic conditions in order to affect the balance between the sexes. They also discard the notion of a universal femininity. Kate Millett in *Sexual Politics* suggests that patriarchy is the sole cause of women's subordination and subjugation. She claims in her "The Theory of Sexual Politics",

> . . . our society, like all other historical civilizations is a patriarchy. That fact is evident at once if one recalls that the military, industry, technology, universities, science political office and finance – in short, every avenue of power within the society, including the coercive force of the police, is entirely in male hands. . . . (Showalter, p. 291).

She attacks sexism in contemporary literature in the works of D.H. Lawrence, Henry Miller, Norman Mailer and Jean Genet. Millett traces sexual politics everywhere in history, psychology, anthropology, religion and literature. Like John Stuart Mill, she concludes that family is the primary and foremost model of all political relationships, which are based on the dominance of the male and the subordination of the female. From social science she borrows the essential distinction between "sex" and "gender". She asserts that "Sex is biological, gender psychological and therefore cultural". She wishes for a time when there will be no monogamous family. She criticizes Freud's theory of penis envy.

Mary Ellman in *Thinking About Women* (1968) has talked about the derogatory stereotypes of women characters in the literature of men. She protests against Walter Peter's "Phallic Criticism". Judith Newton and Deborah Rosenfelt in their *Feminist Criticism and Social Change* (1985) espouse the cause for a materialist feminist criticism, which escapes the tragic essentialism of those feminist critics who project the image of women as universally impotent and universally good.

Elaine Showalter's *A Literature of Their Own* (1977) examines British women authors since the Brontes from the point of view of women's experience. Showalter thinks that a writer's experience is the essential ingredient of her writing. She calls women's writing a sub-culture. She posits three phases in the growth of the feminist tradition: "limitation, protest and self-discovery". The first is the "feminine" phase from 1840 to 1880, which includes authors like Elizabeth Gaskell and George Eliot. The second phase is the "feminist" phase from 1880–1920, which includes authors like Elizabeth Robbins and Olive Schreiner, who are against male values. The third phase is female "female phase" (1920–1980) which includes Rebecca West, Katherine Mansfield and Dorothy Richardson. This is the phase of self-exploration and the search for identity.

Whereas the American feminists of the 1960s had started by vigorously denouncing Freud, the French feminists took it for granted that psychoanalysis could provide an emancipatory theory of the personal and a path to the exploration of the unconscious, both of vital importance to the analysis of the oppression of women in a patriarchal society.

Freud's theory of male superiority and female inferiority was based on biology: the female child, seeing the male organ, recognises herself as female and inferior because she realises that she lacks a penis. According to Freud it is woman's nature to be ruled by man and her sickness to envy him. Farnham and Lundberg also adopt Freud's theory:

> When she discovers that her brother differs from her by possessing an organ she lacks, she comes to the conclusion, for reasons we have indicated, that his entire structure and sphere of activity is superior. (Showalter, p. 234)

Eminent psychoanalyst Clara Thompson criticizes Freud's view:

> Freud never became free from the Victorian attitude toward woman. He accepted as an inevitable part of

> the fate of being a woman the limitation of outlook and life of the Victorian era. . . . The castration complex and penis envy concepts, two of the most basic ideas in his whole thinking are postulated on the assumption that women are biologically inferior to men. (Freidan, p. 260).

W.S. Byatt also rejects Freud's view that a woman can be glorified only in her femininity. She argues for the autonomy, self-fulfilment, self-realisation and independence of women.

In *Psychoanalysis and Feminism* (1975) Juliet Mitchell defends Freud by claiming that "psychoanalysis is not a recommendation for a patriarchal society" but an analysis of one. According to her, Freud is expounding only his theory to illustrate the mental representation of a social reality; he does not defend his social reality. Feminists are opposed to the view of women as "passive, narcissistic, masochistic and penis-envying", suggests Eagleton. However, according to some French feminists, Freud's "penis" or "phallus" is a symbolic concept and not a biological reality. Some French feminist critics such as Helen Cixous, Luce Irigarary and Julia Kristena have started new writing on the problems of women. Jane Gallop says that Lacan's categories of biological distinction seem inevitably to involve a subordination of the female physically. The male is "castrated" by not being the total fullness promised by the phallus, while the female is "castrated" by not being male. In spite of their internal differences, the French feminist critics say that women's subjectivity has emerged from women's physiology and bodily instincts.

The forgoing discussion shows that women in all cultures have suffered under patriarchal hegemony. But the life of African-American women was more miserable, since she had to experience more pain and anguish than other groups of women. She was the triple sufferer, a victim of racism, sexism and classism.

African-American women had participated with White women in the suffrage movement. Nonetheless, the African-

American woman was denied political rights for a long time. Sojourner Truth was one of the first African-American women who fought for the political rights of African-American women. In 1867 on the occasion of the first annual meeting of the American Equal Rights Association, she expressed her desire that African-American women must be granted political rights. Her classic speech, "Arn't I a woman", which she delivered at the Akron Women's Rights Convention in 1851, spurred the African-American women to fight for their rights. Not only, African-American women were deprived of legal opportunities, but they were also denied the right of education. Alice Childress claims that

> We are the only social group within the United States ever forbidden by law to read and write. The law also forbade any White to teach us to read, we and the native Americans were the only citizens or aliens legally forbidden to enter libraries, concert halls, theatres and public schools. In order to change we spent many lives and much money and time. And who allied themselves with us had to pay similar penalties. (qtd. in Parmar, p. 234)

While feminism seems to address the concerns of and speak for all women, in practice it articulates only the concerns of White middle-class women. Barbara Smith points out this bias of feminism in her famous essay, "Toward a Black Feminist Movement":

> Elain Showalter in her review essay on Literary Criticism for *Signs* states that: 'The best work being produced today [in Feminist Criticism] is exacting and cosmopolitan, her essay is neither'. If it were, she would not have failed to mention a single Black or Third World woman writer, whether 'major' or 'minor', to cite her questionable categories. . . . Showalter obviously thinks that the identities of being Black and female are mutually exclusive, as this statement illustrates: 'Furthermore, there are other literary sub-cultures (Black American novelists, for

> example) whose history offers a precedent for feminist scholarship to use. The idea of critics like Showalter *using* Black literature is chilling, a case of barely disguised cultural imperialism. The final insult is that she footnotes the preceding remark by pointing readers to work on Black literature by White males Robert Bone and Roger Rosenblatt. (Newton and Rosenfelt, p. 6)

African-American women realized that the feminist movement did not address their problems and felt rejected from the "main stream of the White feminist movement" (Bhatnagar, p. 314).

African-American men were Black but not female so they did not face gender oppression, and White women were female but not Black so they could not understand the agony of being Black. It is only African-American women who had to confront the twin problems of being Black and being vulnerable women. Neither the African-American movement nor the feminist movement could address their problems fully.

Let us, for example, look at the different roles of men and women defined in a Black Nationalist pamphlet from the early 1970s:

> We understand that it is and has been traditional that the man is the head of the house. He is the leader of the house/nation because his knowledge of the world is broader, his awareness is greater, his understanding is fuller and his application of this information is wiser. . . . After all, it is only reasonable that the man be the head of the house because he is able to defend and protect the development of his home. . . . Women cannot do the same things as men – they are made by nature to function differently. Equality of men and women is something that can not happen even in the abstract world. Men are not equal to other men, i.e., ability, experience, or even understanding. The value of men and women can be

> seen as in the value of gold and silver; they are not equal but both have great value. We must realize that men and women are a complement to each other because there is no house/family without a man and his wife. Both are essential to the development of any life. (Mwananchi, p. 4-5)

The liberation movement of both groups, White women and African-American men, spoke only about their problems and ignored those of African-American women. Despite their great contribution and support to both movements African-American women failed to draw their attention to their plight. The principal objective of this movement was to achieve social equality with affluent White men. Having been marginalized in both these movements, a kind of awareness came to African-American women, an awareness of their work and dignity.

Before the Civil Rights movement only two literary traditions were in vogue, the White American tradition and the African-American male tradition. But since the 1970s the African-American women's literary tradition has also been gaining the requisite validation. The large bulk of work that encompasses African-American women's literature has added a new dimension to African-American literature. That is why Toni Morrison states, "We have spoken of Renaissance before, but this one is ours, not somebody else" (Usha Puri, p. 156).

Barbara Smith seems to speak for all African-American women writers when she talks of the difficulties of initiating a new tradition, the tradition of African-American women writing:

> I do not know where to begin. Long before I tried to write this I realized that I was attempting something unprecedented, something dangerous merely by writing about Black women writers from a feminist perspective and about Black lesbian writers from any perspective at all. These things have not been done. Not by White male critics, expectedly. Not by Black male critics. Not by White women critics who think

> of themselves as feminists. And most crucially not by Black women critics who, although they pay the most attention to Black women writers as a group, seldom use a consistent feminist analysis or write about Black lesbian literature. All segments of the literary world - whether establishment, progression, Black, female or lesbian - do not know, or at least act as if they do not know, that Black women writers and Black lesbian writers exist . . . . This invisibility, which goes beyond everything that either Black men or White women experience and tell about in their writing, is one reason it is so difficult for me to know where to start. It seems overwhelming to break such a massive silence. (Newton and Rosenfelt, p. 3)

Mary Helen Washington laments the scant attention paid to African-American women writing:

> One of the factors contributing to the misconceptions and confusions surrounding the Black women is the treatment of the Black woman writer. Like all Black writers, Black women have never been fairly represented in anthologies - Black or White. They are almost never as well known as Ellison, Wright, Baldwin or Baraka, not to mention White American authors. It is incredible that major Black women novelists such as Toni Morrison, Nella Larsen, Zora Neale Hurston, Gwendolyn Brooks, Dorothy West, Ann Petry, Paule Marshall, Alice Walker and Margaret Walker are almost never taught in college level American literature courses and rarely mentioned in women's studies courses. We are not bemoaning the issue simply because of lack of equal time, but because so many countless generations of men and women have been deprived of the insight and sensitivity of these writers. (pp. IX-X)

In 1973, Walker commented on the indifference and inadequacy of critics in dealing with African-American women writers:

> Critics seem unusually ill-equipped to discuss and analyse the works of Black women intelligently. Generally they do not even make an attempt; they prefer rather to talk about the lives of Black women writers, not about what they write. (qtd. in Viswanathaṇ and Manickam, p. 16)

Apathetic attitudes towards African-American women awakened their sense of self-esteem and consciousness. It signifies a collective awareness of one's own lot as African-American, female and poor. So African-American feminists are always keen to erase the stigma of race, gender and class. They vehemently protest against these inequities. They want to be treated as equal to Whites. According to Patricia Hill Collins, the term African-American feminist applies to primarily those African-American women who possess some vision of feminist consciousness. Critics like Guy Sheftall believe that men can be included within this category. She identifies certain peculiar features of African-American feminist ideas:

> Black women's experience with both racial and gender oppression result in needs and problems distinct from White women and Black men; and as African-Americans. (Viswanathan and Manickam, pp. 15-16)

These women rebel against their ill-treatment, oppression and discrimination and fight for their rights:

> An African-American feminist presence has evolved most obviously in connection with the second wave of the American women's movement beginning in the late 1960s: Black, other Third World and working women have been involved in the feminist movement from its start, but both outside reactionary forces and racism and elitism within the movement itself have served to obscure our participation. In 1973 Black feminists primarily located in New York, felt the necessity of forming a separate Black feminist group. This became the National Black feminist organisation.

> (NBFO). ("A Black Feminist Statement: The Combahee River Collection", p. 14)

The problems before the African-American feminists were manifold and demanded complex responses as has been indicated by Michele Wallace:

> We exist as women who are Black who are feminists, each stranded for the moment, working independently because there is not yet an environment in this society remotely congenial to our struggle – because, being on the bottom, we would have to do what no one else has done: we would have to fight the world. (Michele Wallace, p. 10)

African-American women vehemently opposed issues of inequity, segregation, racism and sexism. African-American feminists spurred African-American women to improve in every respect. They fought to retrieve their lost worth through their art and literature. In writing they followed distinct patterns.

Though African-American women writers made a vital contribution to the development of African-American literature, their efforts were devalued. The discriminated system of writing provoked African-American women writers to undertake a new venture. They have ultimately proved their worth, and their distinctive consciousness called forth an original trend of writing. Before the abolition of slavery some White writers had portrayed the plight of African-American women, but their portrayal lacked depth and did not include the African-American perspective. Even African-American male writers mimicked White writers; they too presented African-American women as the stereotyped women: the obsequious wife, the evil femme fatale, the adoring mother and the powerful grandmother.

The myopic perspective of most male writers has often been a source of negative reactions by African-American women. Key Lindsey points out that neither "the Black movement which is primarily concerned with the liberation of Blacks as a class, nor the feminist movement which is concerned with the oppression of women as a class" has helped the African-American woman to overcome the double oppression because "the Black woman fields herself on the outside of both political entities in spite of the fact that she is the object of both forms of oppression". This predicament of African-American women leads to psychological problems between African-American men and women, which contribute to the turmoil, anger and despair that creep into their personal relationships. It is only the parallel African-American feminist movement, which embodies the realization that African-American women are individuals first and women afterwards, which has helped African-American women to move from "infinity of conscious pain" to "de light at day break" (Puri, p. 70).

Neither African-American men nor White feminists espoused the cause of African-American women. They themselves had to come forward to prove their potential by winning their own battle and securing their own rights. They had to frame their own definition of gender and race oppression. Stephen Henderson writes:

> the contradictions between knowledge and action that surfaced in the Civil Rights and Black Power movements forced sensitive and intelligent women to re-examine their own positions *vis-à-vis* the men and to conclude that they were the victims not only of social injustice, but of a sexual arrogance tantamount to dual colonialism one from without and one from within the Black Community. (Parmar, p. 224)

Despite their significant contribution to the development of African-American literary discourse, African-American women writers received recognition only after a long and arduous struggle. As Harriet Jacobs told her African-American women audience in Boston in 1861, "we have been as invisible to the dominant culture as rain. We have been knowers but we have not been known" (Parmar, p. 231).

Phillis Wheatley, Lucy Terry and Harriet E. Wilson started

the tradition. Wheatley pioneered the tradition of African-American poetry in 1773, Ann Plato paved the way for the essay and Harriet Wilson the novel with *Our Nig* (1859). African-American women writers wrote for themselves. It is the recurring struggle in the tradition of these writers that has been continuing since the nineteenth century. *Our Nig*, the first novel written by an African-American woman, neither got critical attention nor appreciation after it had been published. African-American women writers from 1890 to 1910 were also invisible. According to Gates and Hazel Carby, ". . . Black women have published more works of fiction between 1890 to 1910, than the Black men had published in the previous half-century. Nevertheless, this achievement has been ignored." (p. 7)

On account of being Black and female, African-American women authors found it difficult to get their works published. These specimens of talent and wisdom were marginalized such as Paul Marshall, Alice Walker, Gloria Naylor, Alexis De Veau and Toni Morrison. All these writers followed the path of their pioneer, Zora Neale Hurston who instituted a new age for African-American women writers in the 1940s. These writers continue their quest for self. Nothing can stop them; their works reflect their desperate search for self-identity.

Earlier African-American women authors such as Frances Harper, Jessie Fauset, Ann Petry and Nella Larsen present in their writings African-American women characters, who, they believed, would be liked and admired by White readers. Frances Harper, in her preface to *Iola Leroy*, has written that "her story's mission would not be in vain if it awakens in the hearts of our countrymen a stronger sense of justice and a more Christian like humanity" ("Trajectories of Self-Definition", p. 172). Here Harper has been appealing for justice to African-Americans who were being executed, burnt, raped and deprived of their rights as citizens. She wishes to draw the attention of White readers by making a lady-like version of the heroine, Iola Leroy, whom the Whites could admire although she is Black. During the Harlem

Renaissance another African-American woman author named Jessie Fauset wrote in order to influence the White reader. In the preface to *The Chinaberry Tree* (1931) she has declared that her fiction is about

> "these breathing spells in between spaces where coloured men and women work and live and go their ways in no thought of the problems. What are they like then? So few of the other Americans know." ("Trajectories of Self-Definition", p. 173)

Both the writers, Harper and Fauset, were conscious of the White American mindset regarding African-American people. Nella Larsen (1863–1963) also presented a category of female characters who would be approved by the Whites. For example, her heroine, Helga Crane of *Quick Sand* (1928) mimics the White norms so much that she almost becomes an alien in her own community. Ann Petry, too, creates heroines, who wish to pass for Whites. For instance, Lutie Johnson of *The Street* (1946) loses her original identity because she imitates White women.

We find a remarkable exception to this trend in Zora Neal Hurston. *Their Eyes were Watching God* (1937) marks a radical change in African-American women's novel. It was published eight years after the publication of Nella Larsen's *Passing*. Janie, the female protagonist, belongs to a poor and rural community. She refuses to accept the privileged community status as Mayor Jody Stark's widow and remarries Teacake, who is thirteen years younger than she. He also ill-treats her like her first husband Logan Killieks. After killing Teacake to protect herself, she runs away and comes back home unperturbed by the ugly utterances and insinuations of the local "porch" people. According to critics she is the prototype for female characters like Shug in Alice Walker's *The Colour Purple*, Sula in Morrison's *Sula* and Eva Carada in Gayl Jone's *Eva's Man*. Each of these characters follows in the footsteps of Janie, showing an antipathy towards the conventional role of women as daughter, wife and mother.

Hurston is also the first African-American woman writer

who draws on folklore, myth and the history of African-American people. All her heroines discover their self-fulfilment through community, the search for the symbiotic relationship between man and woman, African-American sorority, and the importance of fidelity in interpersonal relationships. Unlike Jessie Fauset and Nella Larsen, she neither presents the crude bitterness against White society nor employs the "passing" theme or the White emulative motif. The language of her fiction also differs from her contemporaries. Her literary themes and concerns are closely interwoven with her real-life experiences. Her female protagonists constantly strive for self-esteem and emancipation. In its radical envisioning of the self as central and its use of language as a means of exploring the self as female and black, *Their Eyes were Watching God* is a forerunner of fiction of the 1970s and 1980s.

Paule Marshall's first novel, *Brown Girl, Brownstones,* ushered in a new period of female characters in African-American literature. It prefigured the major themes of African-American women's fiction in the 1970s, "the Black woman's potential as a full person and necessarily a major actor on the social, cultural and political issues of our time" (*Black Feminist Criticism,* pp. 103-5). Marshall gave new meaning to African-American womanhood by transforming abused creatures into self-conscious rebels who meet the challenges of the world and seek to define their identity within the context of their own culture.

Due to the Civil Rights movement of the 1960s, a vast change came in the literature of African-American women. For a long time, African-Americans intentionally tried to forget their bitter history. After this Renaissance a new dimension is added to the African-American literary tradition. The writers of this era become anxious to relate their past to the present. The emergence of African-American women writers brings immense change in their perspective, especially in the writings of Alice Walker. She prefers the term womanist to feminist. According to Walker "Womanism" expresses women's concern better than "feminism".

Walker's *Meridian,* one of the most celebrated novels, reflects her strong belief in the Black womanist tenets. It tells the story of the African-American woman in a period of transition, the story of a coming to consciousness and a subsequent development of self and search for authenticity. The first part of the novel describes Meridian's initiation into adulthood and the beginning of her search for her Black woman self. The second part focuses on her renunciation of her child and active participation in the Civil Rights movement. The third and final part deals with her release from sexual bonds with an accent on her great preoccupation with the "survival whole" of her people. Meridian's quest for Black womanhood finally turns into a concern for the survival and wholeness of the entire African-American community. She finds the real meaning of her life in her very attempt to change the present social system for the benefit of all African-Americans, male and female. The transformation she insists on is possible not through violence but through a spiritual awakening.

Meridian, thus emerges as a liberated African-American woman with a hard-won insight into the riddles of life. The novel creates an image of the African-American woman in all her complexity, diversity and depth. Thus, by the mid-1970s African-American women writers such as Paule Marshal, Alice Walker, Gayl Jones, Tonicade Bambara and Toni Morrison have provided a space for the problems of African-American women in their literary writings. And the novels of these writers reveal the pain and suffering of African-American women, which is seen as a distaff literature. These writers aspire to reform the menace of race, gender and class, but finding their voice has not been easy for them, as Barbara Christian has observed:

> To be able to use the range of one's own voice, to attempt to express the totality of self, is a recurring struggle in the tradition of those writers from the nineteenth century to the present. ("Trajectories of Self-Definition", p. 234)

Toni Morrison, too, belongs to the tradition of Paule Marshall, Gloria Naylor, Alice Walker and others. Her fictional writings have a variety of thematic dimensions, and her treatment of contemporary problems has a depth and magnitude not frequently found in other writers' work. Her novels raise the issues of racism, sexism and classism. For instance she sees these issues not as being separate but as interlinked, and her novels deal with these issues together, though the focus varies in each work.

In Toni Morrison's first novel, *The Bluest Eye* (1970), the emphasis is mainly on racial oppression. Morrison demonstrates the influence of European White beauty on the self-image of the African-American female child. Apart from racism, sexism and classism are also evident in this novel, but these two issues are not very prominently dealt. Probably Morrison in the beginning of her career considers radical racial discrimination as the greatest cause of oppression.

The second novel, *Sula* (1973), focuses on gender violence. Morrison is concerned with the struggle for individual rights in general and woman's rights in particular, rather than the rights of African people as a collective group. The third novel, *Song of Solomon* (1977), deals with the issue of class in relation to race and gender. Morrison has now become more conscious of a dialectical connection between capitalism, racism, and sexism.

The fourth novel, *Tar Baby* (1981), is about class struggle. The struggle between the ruling class and the subject class becomes the focal point. In this novel Morrison has shown that racism and sexism emerge from capitalism. Hence capitalism is the basic cause of African-American's oppression.

In Morrison's masterpiece, *Beloved* (1987), the thematic emphasis is on collective class struggle against slavery. It looks into a critical period in the history of African people to illustrate that the economic source of both gender and class exploitation is unobscured in slavery. Sexual assault is regarded as a visible problem, not as it exists between African men and women but as it exists within the context of the economic relationship between master and slave. As sexual exploitation is considered a consequence of the economic exploitation of African people, race oppression is also the result of classism.

Jazz (1992) adds a new dimension to the solution arrived at in *Beloved* with its thematic stress on gender solidarity through women bonding. It is necessary for women to be united. Morrison achieves her objective by transposing Jazz, the music that springs out of her people and expresses their happiness and sadness, their beliefs and their psyche, into another medium, the novel, telling the world the ongoing oppression tale of her folks. Her latest novel, *Paradise* (1997), again reveals the necessity of gender solidarity among women.

Morrison has received a great deal of critical attention since Bessie Jones and Audrey L. Vision's *The World of Toni Morrison: Explorations in Literary Criticism*, the first book length study of Morrison's work. Four others – Karla Holloway and Stephanie Demedrakopolous' *New Dimensions of Spirituality: A Biracial and Bicultural Reading of the Novels of Toni Morrison* (1987), Nellie Mckay, ed., *Critical Essays on Toni Morrison* (1988), Wilfred D. Samuels and Clenora Hudson-Weems, *Toni Morrison* (1990), and Harold Bloom, ed., *Modern Critical Views: Toni Morrison* (1990), followed in quick succession. The critical output on Morrison continued with Trudier Harris' *Fiction and Folklore: The Novels of Toni Morrison* (1991), Barbara Rigney's *The Voices of Toni Morrison* (1991), Doreatha Drummond Mbalia's *Toni Morrison's Developing Class Consciousness* (1991), Patrick Bryce Bjork's *The Novels of Toni Morrison: The Search for Self and Place Within the Community* (1992), Karen Carman's *Toni Morrison's World of Fiction* (1993), Henry Louis Gates Jr., and K. A. Appiah, eds., *Toni Morrison: Critical Perspectives Past and Present* (1993), Denise Heinze's *The Dilemma of "Double-Consciousness": Toni Morrison's Novels* (1993).

These critical studies place Morrison within five contexts: race, gender, class, comparative American/Western literature, and universal paradigms. Feminist critics have focused on how gender shapes Morrison's works; Marxist critics have dwelt on Morrison's class consciousness and cultural redefinitions; comparativists have demonstrated Morrison's debt to outstanding authors such as Faulkner, Joyce, Ellison, Virginia Woolf and Shakespeare; and universalists have discovered patterns such as Christian myth or archetypal psychology in Morrison's fiction. These multifaceted critical approaches to Toni Morrison's fiction are by no means reciprocally exclusive of one another or exhaustive of all possibilities.

The aim of this dissertation is to make an in-depth analysis of the interconnectedness of race, gender and class in the novels of Toni Morrison with a view to establishing a growing pattern in her work and helping obtain fresh insights into her fictional art.

1

The Bluest Eye: Conformity Leading to Defeat

The migration of African-Americans from the South to the North and to the Central Midwest posed several problems such as racial and social adjustment, class differentiation, and above all a loss of identity. Right from the first day of slavery they were judged by Whites as sub-human on the basis of their dark complexion. Thus the oppressive story of racism began in America, which generated immense pain, sorrow, bloodshed, death and, above all, the negation of a whole race. Race conflict critically affected the lives of African-Americans. As Toni Morrison has aptly asserted:

> That which was 'White' (or Anglo, male, Christian wealthy) was extolled and infused with connotations of benevolence and superiority while that which was not White (or not Anglo, female or Christian poor) was debased and associated with malevolence and inferiority. (Braxton and McLavghlin, p. 153).

To have dark skin meant to suffer inequities in the White America where Whites were considered superior, more intelligent and virtuous than African-Americans.

Racism coupled with sexism proved to be more oppressive for African-American women. Owing to their complexion and sex they had to confront double atrocities. They were sexually exploited by both African-American as well as White men. Being black, African-American women face racism, and being female they are the victims of sexism. So "To be black and female was to be in double jeopardy" (Frances, p. 90).

Morrison understands real beauty and considers the lure of physical charm:

> When the strength of a race depends on its beauty, when the focus is turned to how one looks as opposed to what one is, we are in trouble. . . . The concept of physical beauty as a virtue is one of the dumbest, most pernicious and destructive ideas of the Western world, and we should have nothing to do with it. Physical beauty has nothing to do with our past, present or future. Its absence or presence was only important to "them" the white people who used it for anything they wanted. ("Behind the Making of the Black Book", p. 89)

She understands the ultimate reality of physical beauty, which is transient and perishable.

The adverse effect of racism has been presented in *The Bluest Eye,* which is set in a small Midwestern town of Lorain in Ohio during the Depression. It focuses on a love starved girl, Pecola Breedlove, an eleven-year-old African-American girl who believes that she is ugly and longs for blue eyes as a symbol of beauty which could bring her admiration, respect and happiness. The story—desire of an African-American girl for a pair of blue eyes—is a symbolic statement about the conflict between societal values of the Anglo-American and the Afro-American cultures. It also reflects the effect on the psyche of the people within those cultures. The longing for blue eyes symbolises the African-American woman's yearning for impossible White ideals.

The novel presents the story of the Breedlove family. The narrator, Claudia Mcteer, the younger daughter of Mcteer, narrates the story of her friend and classmate, Pecola Breedlove. In telling the story of Pecola and her family she uses her own stable family as a point of comparison and contrast. The novel begins with a grownup Claudia reflecting on the events that took place between the Falls of 1940 and 1941. In her mind that year is fixed as the strange ominous one when marigolds did not sprout. Morrison makes use of this nature image as a major structural element to divide the book into four sections/seasons—autumn, winter, spring, summer—reflecting ironically, on the tragedy of Pecola Breedlove. The four seasons here take a diagonal approach, as the year here does not begin in January or in Spring but in Fall. The reason for autumn to be the starting point of the story is that Pecola's story does not follow the usual mythic cycle of birth, death and re-birth or the planting - harvest - planting cycle. Instead it proceeds from pathos to tragedy and ultimately to madness.

Since her childhood Pecola suffers from an inferiority complex that she is ugly and thus unlovable. She lacks self-esteem, and she thinks that she can win love and respect of people only if she could become pretty and beautiful. She yearns for a pair of blue eyes, and this yearning soon becomes an obsession with her. Her obsession for blue eyes makes her believe in fairy tales and other magical stories. It is Cinderella's aspiration to be changed from a char girl to the belle of the ball or Sleeping Beauty waiting a hundred years for the prince to awaken her from slumber. This is a failed tale of the ugly duckling who turned into a beautiful swan. Pecola is never successful in her attempts. She

> seems doomed whatever she does—if she resorts to fantasy, she is considered crazy, and if she tries to live in the real world, there is no place for her—her desire for blue eyes ties her to several heroines of fairy tales and to many young girls who have wished for features other than the ones they have. (Harris, p. 73)

Like Pecola, her parents Cholly and Pauline too suffer from a sense of inferiority complex. They do not know the meaning of love, and they are not able to instill in their children a positive self-identity, for they have none of their own. Cholly had a very unfortunate and unhappy experience while growing up, and these experiences have a distorting influence on her personality. An orphan since his childhood, he was looked after by an old aunt Jimmy. Her untimely death left him anchorless in this world. Unloved and uncared for he grows up without learning the meaning of love, compassion and kindness. Further, as a teenager he suffers humiliation at the hands of the White men who catch him in the act of making love. His marriage to Paulin also proves disastrous as both of them are not only unsuited to each other but are also incapable of giving love. Pauline too has a miserable childhood, and she too has grown up unloved and uncared for.

The custom of nicknaming is a popular tradition in the African-American community, which is helpful in creating a person's image. Pecola's mother, Pauline, is distressed for not having any nickname from her relatives and family. She "never felt at home anywhere, or that she belonged any place" (p. 86). Being frustrated she starts ignoring her family and community, which is why she starts seeking love and adulation in her master's home from where she gets a nickname 'Polly'—they "gave her what she never had" (p. 99). Bernine Regan has written that to be called by one's own name has a negative impact, whereas a nickname makes a positive impact on the psychology of a person, which is why Pauline was unhappy not to have any nickname. Only Claudia and her sister were exceptions, for their parents allow them to be friends with Pecola.

It is the White criterion of beauty that denies Pecola a positive sense of self. Owing to her light complexion and green eyes her friend, Maureen Peal, gets preferential treatment and admiration from teachers and friends. She has a sense of superiority because of her light colour, and she loses no opportunity to make fun of Pecola: "I am cute! and you ugly! African-American and ugly black emos. I am cute" (p. 56). Other African-American girls of her class tease and harass her. They form a group and poke fun at her by singing in chorus, "Black emo. Black emo yadaddsleepsnekked. Black emo black emo ya dadd sleeps nekked. Black emo . . . " (p. 50). Pecola begins to believe that she is ugly and that people avoid and ignore her because of her dark colour:

> He does not see her, because for him there is nothing to see. . . . She does not know what keeps his glance suspended. . . . But she has seen interest, disgust, even anger in grown male eyes. . . . It is the blackness that accounts for, that creates, the vacuum edged with distaste in white eyes. (pp. 36-37)

The reason that African-Americans harass other African-Americans is due, perhaps, due to the self-denigration induced by White hegemony. White standards have corrupted the minds of African-American people, and consequently they have developed self-hatred.

. Whenever Pecola goes to buy candy from Yocobowski's store, she feels that he avoids looking at her. It is as if her very presence or existence were denied and negated:

> She looks up at him and sees the vacuum where curiosity ought to lodge. And something more. The total absence of human recognition the glazed separateness. (36)

The absence of human recognition Pecola finds in Yocobowski's glance reinforces her own negative self-perception. For her these encounters grow very painful and frightening. The most horrible rejection occurs when a young boy named Louis Junior plays a cruel hoax on her. Louis invites her to his mother's house to show her some kittens. Instead of showing them he throws his mother's cat at her. The frightened cat scratches and bruises her face. After that, he throws the cat flying into the radiator and blames Pecola for killing it. Geraldine, the mother, infuriated not as much as by the death of the cat, as by the presence of an African-American girl in her home, lashes out at Pecola in words that cut deeper than the cat's claws: "Get out. . . . You nasty little African-American bitch. Get out of my house". (p. 72) What is ironical here is the mimicking of White values and attitudes by the African-American woman herself.

The ultimate act of brutalisation and betrayal for Pecola comes when her own father, Cholly, rapes her and makes her pregnant. Consequently the baby dies.

Pecola makes efforts to come to terms with the world by saying prayers without fail. She seeks the help of a magician who gives her false assurance of getting her eyes changed into blue ones. She thinks that by possessing blue eyes she will become beautiful and hence acceptable to and loved by all. Her obsession with blue eyes soon makes her slip into a state of insanity in which she comes to believe that she has got blue eyes and has become beautiful.

Pecola's madness, coupled with the history of her family's madness, excites scorn rather than sympathy. This novel also conveys how history, like individual life, is ultimately incoherent. The entire society is caught up in the same futile cycle of despair. It is only because of the absence of self-love and self-worth that the characters separate from their tradition. Due to the lack of such communal coherence and kinship ties, they have little impetus to grow and survive. For instance, the portrayal of Cholly's character arouses our pity and sympathy and makes us condone to some extent his rape of Pecola. The implicit argument shows that social forces have conspired to produce the sort of man represented by Cholly. Pauline is alienated due to her aping of the White bourgeois social model. Even in her childhood she never experiences a sense of belonging to any place. Her White patron gives her a nick name "Polly" which identifies her as "the ideal servant". Mrs. Foster, a White woman, advises Pauline to break off with Cholly because of his abusive treatment of her. But she continues her relationship with him because she thinks that it is not good to leave an African-American man for a White woman. This addresses the conflict between African-American women and White women. Here we find that racial solidarity forces Pauline to live with Cholly and endure his abuse, whereas her financial condition forces her to carry on with her job at the White master's house. Pauline becomes the victim of White beauty and romantic love:

> Along with the idea of romantic love, she [Pauline] was introduced to another physical beauty. Probably the most destructive ideas in the history of human thought. Both originated in envy, thrived in insecurity and ended in disillusion. (Gibson, p. 154)

Pecola's parents never try to develop a positive relationship with her. Still she thinks that blue eyes will make her different and give her the love and security that are desperately missing from her life. For her, blue eyes are a panacea for all her miseries:

> It had occurred to Pecola sometime ago that if her eyes were different. . . . Those eyes that held the pictures, and knew the sights – if those eyes of hers she herself would be different. . . . If she looked different and beautiful, may be [her father] would be different, and [her mother] too. May be they'd say, "Why, look at pretty-eyed Pecola, we mustn't do bad things in front of those pretty eyes". (p. 34)

So Pecola's ultimate ambition is to have a pair of blue eyes. And she is quite hopeful of possessing them someday despite severe odds. To have something wonderful would take a long "long time".

Equally significant is the physical violence done to the African-American child by parents who are in themselves confused about their identity as in the case of the Breedloves. By portraying the "grotesque violence" done to children, Morrison explained, she was trying to depict "the nature and relationship between parental love and violence. Parents do violence to their children everyday". (Samuels and Hudson, p. 16) How can a community interact in a mutual frenzy of blind identity to mutilate people, especially girls and women? In this novel Morrison's stress is on the society, not on the family unit. In her view the African-American's self-image is ruined at a tender age owing to the White standard of beauty. So the outward appearance is more important than inner qualities.

Like Pecola, Claudia and Frieda also face the same world. Still their response is different from hers. Her biggest sin is to be born African-American and female. We sympathize with Pecola when Mrs. Mcteer scolds her for drinking three quarts of milk in one day. Claudia states that Pecola "took every opportunity to drink milk out of it just to handle and see sweet Shirley's face" (p. 16). But her excess love for the cup also shows her love for a white complexion. She longs for self-respect as a means of imposing order on the chaos of her world. A sense of self-worth and stability are unavailable to her in the familial and wider environment, so she creates a subjective world of illusion. She resides in a brutal world of rejection, deprived of even parental love. The rapport between mother and daughter is so distant that Pecola invariably thinks of her mother as "Mrs. Breedlove".

Pecola's isolation is complete when she retreats into her own world of insanity. In this utopia she gets a new friend who makes her believe that she has the bluest eyes in the world, for which she has been praying for a year: "Each night, without fail, she prayed for blue eyes. Fervently, for a year she had prayed". (p. 35)

Soaphead Church drives Pecola mad, not only by physically abusing the child who is now pregnant by her own father but by convincing her that she has the pair of blue eyes. When she comes to Soaphead, he makes the sign of the cross over her. He gives her the poisoned meat and tells her to feed it to the dog to get blue eyes. He says, "If nothing happens, you will know that God has refused you. If the animal behaves strangely, your wish will be granted on the day following this one". (p. 139)

Pecola does as she is instructed and feeds the dog. And she is sure that she has got the blue eyes. She exemplifies the path of those who will never be able to recover, the ultimate victims who will never be able to speak for themselves.

Toni Morrison has been a consistently insightful and helpful critic of her own writing. In this novel she has indicated that her aim was to take love and the effect of its scarcity in the world as her major themes focusing on the interior lives of her characters, especially those within an enclosed society. Her motto is to show "how to survive whole in a world where we are all of us in some measure, victims of something". (Klotman, p. 90)

The entire emphasis of the novel is on racism, which

> abstracts the colour of the living body into non-colours of extreme value, African-American and White, within this organization; African-American represents the shade of evil, the devil's aspect, night, separation, loneliness, sin, dirt, excrement, the inside of the body, and White represents the mark of good, the token of innocence, purity, cleanliness, spirituality, virtue and hope. (Kovel, p. 232)

The theme of the novel is that racism devastates the self-image of the African-American female in general and African-American female children in particular. Though Morrison emphasizes racism as the primary shackle confronting African-American people, the issue of class is also not untouched. As Donald B. Gibson observes, "the novel has its class ramification too" (Gibson, p. 171)

Pecola is not only the victim of race and gender but of class also. She is destitute but the Macteer family, which takes her in, is better off. The divergence between the Macteer house and the White house where Pecola's mother works is not the comparison between African-American and White only but between destitution and affluence also. "Our house [Macteer's] is old, cold and green. At night a kerosene lamp lights one large room. The others are braced in darkness, peopled by roaches and mice. . . ." (p. 5)

> Right before the entrance to the park was the large White house with the wheelbarrow full of flowers. Short crocus blades sheathed the purple – and –

> white hearts that so wished to be first they endured the chill and rain of early spring. . . . We circled the proud house and went to the back. (p. 82)

Pecola's quest for self becomes fruitless. She fails in her mission:

> Her struggle towards selfhood take place in infertile soil leading, in the final analysis, to a life and sterility. Like the marigold planted by Claudia, Pecola could not grow. (Samuels and Hudson, p. 13).

Claudia like a clairvoyant understands the cause of Pecola's tragic end. She speaks of the cause of her tragedy:

> Quiet as it's kept, there were no marigolds in the fall of 1941. We thought, at the time, that it was because Pecola was having her father's baby that the marigolds did not grow. A little examination and much less melancholy would have proved to us that our seeds were not the only ones that did not sprout; nobody's did. . . .
>
> It was a long time before my sister and I admitted to ourselves that no green was going to spring from our seeds. Once we knew, our guilt was relieved only by fights and mutual accusations about who was to blame. For years I thought my sister was right: It was my fault. . . . It never occurred to either of us that the earth itself might have been unyielding. (p. 3)

And she finishes:

> And now when I see her searching the garbage - for what? The thing we assassinated? . . . I even think now that the land of the entire country was hostile to marigolds that year. This soil is bad for certain kinds of flowers. Certain seeds it will not nurture, certain fruit it will not bear, and when the land kills of its own violation, we acquiesce and say the victim had no right to live. We are wrong, of course, but

> it doesn't matter. It's too late. At least on the edge of my town, among the garbage and the sunflowers of my town, it's much, much, much too late. (pp. 163-64)

Claudia and Frieda, brought up in positive circumstances, therefore have a more positive psychological reaction to the situation, whereas Pecola, brought up in confused and negative circumstances, shows an absolutely confused and negative attitude to life.

Towards the end of the novel Claudia, now a more mature person, blames the entire society for having failed to love Pecola. The society always disparages her importance as a human being. The White patriarchal American society is responsible for making Pecola aberrant and psychologically unhealthy. The society forces her to think that she is worthless and ugly. And this is why she loses her mental balance. On the contrary Claudia can sustain herself because she saves herself from the adverse effect of the White Euro-centric standard. She was taught by her parents' survival technique, which Pecola's parents never give to their children. Lack of proper guidance and co-operation becomes the cause of her failure in her quest.

Morrison, through her strong narrative voice, delivers a sensitive delineation of the intolerable plight of African-American life. She shows not only race consciousness in the novel but also the economic exploitation of African-American people. For instance, *The Bluest Eye* begins with three versions of the "Dick and Jane" reader prevalent in public schools at the time (the 1940s) of the novel. It is a very significant and symbolical passage. Through these passages Morrison has tried to reflect the ironic duality of the school and home experience. The first paragraph shows the world of the middle class, secure, suburban and White, complete with dog, cat, non-working mother and leisurely father. It has simple sentences, but later on it is repeated without punctuation and a third time words are jumbled together:

> Here is the house. It is green and white. It has a red

> door. It is very pretty. Here is the family, Mother, father Dick and Jane live in the green and - white house. They are very happy. See Jane. She has a red dress. She wants to play. Who will play with Jane? See the cat. It goes meow-meow. Come play. Come play with Jane. The kitten will not play. See Mother. Mother is very nice. Mother, will you play with Jane? Mother laughs. Laugh, Mother laugh. See father. He is big and strong. Father, will you play with Jane? Father is smiling. Smile, father, smile. See the dog. Bowwow goes the dog. Do you want to play with Jane? See the dog run. Run, dog, run. Look, look. Here comes a friend, the friend will play with Jane. They will play a good game. Play, Jane, play. (p. 1)

The second version is the replica of the first, giving the exact message, as it lays out the manifest, simple, synthetic world of the storybook. This version is without capitals and punctuation, yet the words are recognizable:

> Here is the house it is green and white it has a red door it is very pretty here is the family mother father Dick and Jane live in the green and - white house they are very happy see Jane she has a red dress she wants to play who will play with Jane see the cat it goes meow-meow come play come play with Jane . . . play Jane play. (p. 1)

In spite of its similarities, the last version lacks spaces and punctuation. It is wholly run together and appears like one long collection of consonants and vowels seeming to signify nothing. This version reflects the psychic chaos of the novel:

> Here is the house it is green and white it has ared door it is very pretty here is the family mother father dick and janelive in the green and white house they are very happy see janesheh asareddress she want stop lay who will play with janeseethecatit goes me owmeowcome play come play with jane . . . play janeplay. (p. 2)

The very first version signifies an alien White world, represented by the Fisher family that violates the lives of the African-American children. The second version shows the lifestyle of the two African-American children, Claudia and Frieda, who have loving and supportive parents who despite their financial hardship try their best to survive and cope with world. And the third paragraph indicates the disturbed life of the Breedlove family. Their daughter Pecola, whose family mutilates her mentally, survives in a deformed world. In the third version individual space evaporates as it does in the novel. The father meddles and distorts the child's space. Pecola's life is smashed as it was indirectly reflected in the last version:

> The cat and dog motif appears in a sinister form in the novel. The black cat blue eyes, the blue eyes haunt Pecola, and the dog writhes as it dies of poison, the sign that Pecola must look for in order that her eyes become blue. Then Pecola, who is Jane of the First Grade Reader, invents the friend who comes to play with her as she enters the world of insanity. (Ranveer, p. 208)

In this novel Morrison's emphasis is chiefly on racism, but covertly she presents issues of class and gender discrimination, other primary obstacles for African-American people. Pecola is oppressed not only due to racism but also due to classism and sexism. Associated with her condition are violence, ugliness and poverty, symbolized by her storefront house.

2

Sula: Failed Rebellion

Toni Morrison sets out in her novels to recover the African-American female self, which is mutilated, fragmented or blotted out. Hence the search for identity is the predominant theme in her novels. Each of her novels stresses the need for self-discovery and self-identity leading to self-actualization. She believes that Afro-American women are different from others:

> There is something inside [them] that makes [them] different from other people. It is not like men and it is not like white woman. (Parker, p. 255)

White women at least get support from their men, while African-American women are isolated and have no one to lean on:

> And she had nothing to fall back on, not maleness not whiteness, not ladyhood, not anything. And out of the profound dissolution of her reality. She may very well have invented herself. ("What the Black Woman Thinks", p. 14)

In Morrison's fiction identity is always provisional. Her female characters combat against three different kinds of oppression – Whiteness, maleness and bourgeois culture – and search desperately for their genuine selves.

By the time of her second novel, *Sula*, Morrison considers a twofold predicament: the effect of racism upon African-American identity formation and the effect of racism and sexism upon the identity formation of the African-American female. In an interview conducted by Colette Dowling, she suggests that "blacks, if they are to succeed in American society, must leave their native communities, and in so doing, cut themselves off from their old lives". (Dowling, p. 58).

Sula explores the theme of twin atrocities of race and gender further, even though her main focus is mainly on gender. Thus in *Sula*, Morrison's focus shifts to the African-American woman as an individual, struggling towards freedom and selfhood. Sula, the central figure of this novel, rejects the traditional norms of feminine respectability like family, marriage, children, grand parental care, sexual mores and the concept of steady job. She hates to see a woman only as a wife, mother, and daughter. In *Sula* Morrison attempts to show the individuality of an African-American woman, struggling for emancipation and identity.

Sula is basically a woman's novel because a woman character dominates the entire novel. The male characters play no prominent role. Most of them are "superficial, immature, untrustworthy and anonymous as is suggested by their names—Jude (Judas) Green (Naive), Boy Boy (infantile), Chicken Little (fearful and diminutive), the Deweys (anonymous)" (Samuels and Hudson, p. 46).

The negative aspects of the male names are most visible when juxtaposed with the empowering names of the women. Every man leaves a community of abandoned women. This abandonment becomes the impetus for Eva, the paradigmatic woman who rebounds through assertiveness and self-reliance after she and her children are deserted by her spouse.

The exploitation of African-American women in America especially in the first quarter of the twentieth century is documented throughout the novel. Morrison's manner of exploring the nature of woman's maltreatment is unique. She has created two female characters—Nel and Sula—and none is complete in herself. The idea that Nel and Sula represent two faces of a coin reverberates through the entire novel. When Sula comes back to the Bottom, Nel thinks that her friend's return is like "getting an eye back" and that talking to Sula has always been "a conversation with herself". Significant too is the authorial comment: "their friendship was so close, they themselves had difficulty distinguishing one's thoughts from the other's". (p. 83) Nel and Sula then are separate facets or faces of one being. Morrison suggests that to attain an ideal and holistic personality, "the part embodied in Sula has to be wedded to the safe conventional part represented by Nel". (Banyiwa, p. 28)

For Nel and Sula the problem of losing their individuality is a direct consequence of the Bottom's limiting definition of women as subservient self-sacrificing beings. Nel follows the traditional role the community prescribes and maintains her social identity, although her personal identity is non-existent. Sula comparatively is a free-spirited woman whose tenaciousness to prove her worth places her at odds with the culturally rich African-American society. In their search for completeness both girls find their world rife with contradictions and tensions. As M. L. Montgomery observes Nel and Sula "experience a profound sense of alienation in a patriarchal world which evolves no terms for their existence" (Montgomery, p. 132).

Morrison's most powerful statement regarding the degradation of the female comes in a paragraph that appears after the first interaction of Nel and Sula:

> Because each had discovered years before they were neither white nor male and that all freedom and triumph was forbidden to them they had set about creating something else to be. (p. 52)

This statement shows both the dilemma and solution of the novel. African-American women are oppressed, and in order to escape their oppression they must become self-propagators. As a contemporary novel on female bonding *Sula* "offers a view of female psychological development that defies traditional male-centred interpretations of female development and calls out for an expansion of the woman-centred paradigm". (Gillespie and Kubitschek, p. 137)

Sula basically deals with the friendship between two girls, Nel Wright and Sula Peace, who face the tremendous contradictions of life. Their broken and scattered lives reveal the depth of their pain, which is the outcome of their loss of identity:

> Their broken friendship is a measure of their broken lives that are cramped from the very start. As counterpoints all the other women in this book (*Sula*) must either fit themselves into the place life has set for them or defy it with tragic circumstances proportionate to their degree of non-accommodation. (Christian, p. 27-28)

Nel and Sula seek solace in each other's company for they share the common ties of being young, African-American and female in a world that is commonly geared to meet the designs of mature White men. Despite having different social backgrounds both are intimate friends because "they found in each other's eyes the intimacy they were looking for" (52).

Their friendship develops at the age of twelve. Each one gets from the other security, love and identity blatantly denied to them in their own homes. Barbara Smith comments that their friendship is "the necessary bonding that has always taken place between Black women for the barest survival. Together the two girls can find the courage to create themselves". (p. 168)

Sula and Nel complement each other. Both are Morrison's favourite characters since they are symbolic of the good and the evil persistently present in the society:

> Yet she [Sula] and Nel are very much alike. They complement each other. They support each other. I suppose the two of them together could have made a wonderful single human being. They are like a Janus head. (Parker, p. 253)

Though both develop a strong bond, they stand poles apart in several respects. Sula is recalcitrant and intrepid, whereas Nel is conventional and homely. Nel becomes a slave to racism and sexism; Sula becomes a liberated woman. She vehemently refuses to accept the traditional role of a woman. She searches for a more meaningful life. She is an iconoclast who hardly bothers with moral codes. She refuses to get married and settle down as a housewife. Sula believes that marriage annihilates the individuality of African-American women to such an extent that they die "like a stump". (p. 143)

For insulting the women of Medallion she comes to their church functions scantily attired, purchases and picks over their food, and "tries out" and rejects their husbands. She condemns the way men have defined natural vocations for women only as mothers or prostitutes. She is a radical feminist who wants to end all kinds of discrimination on the basis of race and gender. She "believes that she can create an identity for herself and that she exists beyond the community and social expectations". ("Towards a Black Feminist Criticism", p. 130)

Sula is aware of the need for "something else to be" and to "rely solely on herself". The novel is named after her, but without her alter ego, Nel, she is incomplete. In spite of having different familial backgrounds, they develop a strong bond of friendship. Nel's family is quite different from Sula's family. Her mother, Helene Sabat, is absolutely conventional while Sula's mother Hannah is not. Nel gets married to Jude Green out of sheer pity for his plight. She devotes her life to Jude and her three children, and yet her marriage is destroyed when Sula returns to Medallion and seduces Nel's husband. Nel knows that she will have no other relationship with men. With Jude she has a sense of identity. That is why after her separation from Jude, she becomes "thighs (that) were truly empty" (p. 110). As Byernar has rightly noted, "the loss of Jude is the loss of identity and the loss of life. . . . [Nel] now becomes a woman without a man and unable to raise her eyes. . ." (qtd. in Samuel and Hudson, p. 45).

Several years after Sula's death, Nel realizes the significance of her friendship. She admits and laments, "We was girls together. . . . O Lord, Sula. . . . girl, girl, girl girl girl" (p. 174).

Sula is a libertine. She feels that men are simply to be used and discarded; perhaps it is in her genes. Her mother, Hannah, is also a seducer. After the death of her husband, Rekus, she refuses to marry again but takes a number of lovers, mostly the spouses of her friends and neighbours. She does not need to develop any close relationship with anyone:

> Hannah's friendship with women were, of course, seldom and short-lived, and the newly-married couples whom her mother took in soon learned what a hazard she was. She could break up a marriage before it had even become one. . . . What she wanted, after Rekus died, and what she succeeded in having more often than not, was some touching everyday. (p. 44)

Sula's behaviour shocks the whole community and her friendship turns into enmity. She is a "living criticism of the dreadful lives of resignation other women live" (Smith, p. 168). When she returns to her home town, her granny Eva asks her about her marriage, to which she replies "I don't want to make somebody else. I want to make myself" (p. 92).

In order to find and realize her true self, she leaves Medallion for a decade. Her daring action makes her a recluse and outcast, but unfortunately she is a failure in her mission. She is unable to obtain anything in love. She is rejected by Ajax, whom she loves sincerely. She becomes possessive and starts to make herself physically beautiful but not mentally. Ajax after realizing this deserts her. Wade Gayles comments: "[Sula] has finally internalized the assumptions about women's role and behaviour in relationship with men, and she has ended her journey toward selfhood" (qtd. in Ray, p. 93).

Her quest is an inward search through which she secures only a sad knowledge of her alienation and loss. Yet we cannot say that she is completely defeated. After her separation from Ajax she feels calm and relaxed and bears a "can't careless" attitude. Nel has once heard her childhood friend declaring:

> My lonely is *mine* . . .
> Your lonely is somebody else's. (p. 143)

It does not matter whether Sula becomes successful or a failure, but she always strives to realize her selfhood. She fights against the prevalent disparity, atrocities and exploitation of society. Since her childhood she has been a dashing, intrepid and bold girl. As Trudier Harris has aptly said *Sula* is antithetical to the basic premise of the fairy story, and "There is little passivity in *Sula,* and innocence is not treasured;. indeed, as is typical of Morrison's girl/woman" (Harris, p. 54).

She is ten times more rebellious than other Morrison characters of, but in spite of her bizarre behaviour, the society needs her:

> Just as the Black in Lorain needed Pecola so that they could nurture a sense of their superiority, so the Blacks in Medallion, Ohio, hating and fearing Sula, improve their behaviour in an unconscious effort to prove their goodness in contrast to her wickedness. (Turner, p. 364)

Sula is presented as a very daring character who can do anything for her emancipation and selfhood. She also helps her friend, Nel, to be conscious of her rights and freedom. For fulfilling her dreams she has to pay a heavy price. Yet she tries her best to create her identity. She is "the modern preternaturally sensitive but rudely thwarted black girl in today's society", (Bischoff, p. 21).

Like a young girl she so startles the society with her extreme emotional impulses that her growth into a "strange, strong and independent woman" is all but predictable. She rejects "behavioural standard of all kinds" and tries to "rely solely on herself". Thus unlike Pecola, Sula lives out her own fantasies, creates her own realities, and gets her own personal objectives. In short, she is motivated by a firm sense of "Me-ness".

The profundity of Sula's defiance is a reflection of the sharp contrast between who she is and what the Bottom decrees for its women. Thus,

> Sula is a pariah whose values are often the polar opposites of those adopted by her provincial society. She becomes a pariah precisely because she rejects those values that aim at uniformity and stifle the self. (Banyiwa, p. 31)

Although Morrison is successful in her treatment of Sula's rebelliousness, she is less convincing in her depiction of the impact that racism and sexism have on Sula's defiance. She writes of Sula's discovery that being neither White nor male means denial of "freedom and triumph". But a careful reading of the novel shows that Morrison's stress is on sexism.

Morrison's focus in *Sula* is on the battle of Black people for individual and racial freedom. They fight to lead a respectable and honorable life. Racial issues are interwoven into the fabric of the novel. The history of Bottom and the lack of development of the Deweys are classic examples of racism. The story of Bottom's origin fits a classic tale of African-American people being deceived by the White master:

> A good White farmer promised freedom and a piece of bottom land to his slave if he would perform some very difficult chores. When the slave completed the work, he asked the farmer to keep his end of the bargain. Freedom was easy — the farmer had no objection to that. But he didn't want to give up any land. So he told the slave that he was very sorry that he had to give him valley land. He had hoped to give him a piece of the Bottom. The slave blinked

> and said he thought valley land was bottom land. The master said, "Oh, no! See those hills? That's bottom land, rich and fertile."
>
> "But it's high up in the hills", said the slave.
>
> "High up from us," said the master, "but when God looks down, it's the bottom. That's why we call it so. It's the bottom of heaven—best land there is."
>
> So the slave pressed his master to try to get him some. He preferred it to the valley. And it was done. The nigger got the hilly land, where planting was backbreaking, where the soil slid down and washed away the seeds, and where the wind lingered all through the winter.
>
> Which accounted for the fact that White people lived on the rich valley floor in that little river town in Ohio, and the Blacks populated the hills above it, taking small consolation in the fact that everyday they could literally lookdown on the white folks. (p. 5)

We find two archetypes of African-American folklore: the White farmer is an imposter and fraud, and the African-American folk are the suffering and deceived ones. This tale shows that it is always the lot of African-American people to be deceived and suffer humiliation. As Daryl C. Dance has observed in the discussion of etiological tales in *Shuckin and Livin* (1978) and elsewhere,

> the black man will always receive the reward of lesser value . . . . despite its occasional strangenesses—the last laugh is really on the Whites, because they have not been able to destroy the will to survive of those blacks up in the Bottom. (Dance, p. 56)

So they are determined to live at any cost. This structure forms the background against which to view the actions of the characters like Sula. The main purpose of writing this novel is to unveil the damaging effect of White values upon the stability of the African-American family in general and African-American women in particular. In the opinion of people marriage is obligatory and necessary. A woman is incomplete and powerless without a man. Morrison debunks this notion in *Sula.* For instance Nel's marriage to Jude distorts her own selfhood. While Sula is a bete-noire in terms of the conventional life, like a masculine figure she seeks physical satisfaction with more and more men. Nel loses the strong love bond with Sula, who always helps and encourages to have. self-confidence. She loses that priceless bond of interdependence, which she shares only with her crony Sula. She regrets:

> "All that time, all that time, I thought I was missing Jude." And the loss passed down on her chest and came up into her throat. "We was girls together," she said as though explaining something. "O Lord, Sula," she cried, "girl, girl, girlgirlgirl." (p. 174)

At the end of the novel she confesses that without Sula she has become the most alienated human being. It is the loss of Sula, which is irreparable.

Let us refer to another example of racial discrimination in the novel. When Nel's mother Helene is going to New Orleans with Nel to attend the death ceremony of her mother, she is publicly humiliated by a conductor. Instead of showing any reaction Helene gives an artificial smile, as if nothing has happened: "Helene smiled. Smiled dazzlingly and coquettishly at the Salmon coloured face of the conductor," and Nel the narrator carefully watches the expression of other passengers:

> She saw the muscles of their faces tighten, a movement under the skin from blood to marble. No change in the expression of the eyes, but a hard wetness that veiled them as they looked at the stretch of her mother's foolish smile. (pp. 21-22)

By this hypocritical action, Helene covers her own racial oppression and insult. Her inordinate respect for the white complexion shows the adverse effect of whiteness. Helene has assimilated White values, yet despite her trappings of a lady, she finds that she continues to be badly treated at the hands of the White people. She has antipathy for her own people and race. The only time she talks with an African woman is to know the whereabouts of the toilet:

> So intense was her distress she finally brought herself to speak about her problem to a black woman with four children who had got on in Tuscaloosa. (p. 23)

This incident leaves a deep imprint on Nel's mind. Hence she starts seeking her identity: "I'm me. I'm not their daughter. I'm not Nel, I'm me. Me" (p. 28). And its effect remains with Nel life-long. She cultivates an intimate relationship with Sula despite the objection of her mother.

Like *The Bluest Eye, Sula* too raises the issues of gender, race and class, but the main focus is on sexism. There are similarities between Pecola Breedlove and Sula Peace. Both yearn to have their own identity. Pecola goes mad while Sula becomes a recluse and pariah. Pecola mentally dies while Sula physically dies. Toni Morrison once again has presented in the novels the hapless lot of African-American women.

3

Song of Solomon: Coming of Age

Morrison has reiterated the theme of the maltreatment of African-Americans in *Song of Solomon.* She seems more conscious of the dialectical relationship among capitalism, racism and sexism in this novel. Morrison deals with the themes of initiation and quest for family roots, which in turn are linked to the search for an African-American cultural heritage. The protagonist of *Song of Solomon,* unlike her previous two novels, is an African-American male, Milkman Dead. Morrison's focus in the third novel also becomes more externally directed, moving beyond the intimacy of the enclosed communities found in her first two novels.

Song of Solomon gives an interesting example of the manner in which equations of power and the levels of class, gender and race operate in a literary work. It is written from a male vantage point. Still, gender oppression of the female emerges as an issue of prominence with the exception that the focus of attention is more on the middle-class African-American woman. The only difference we find between the third novel and its two predecessors is the lesser degree of physical abuse directed toward the African-American woman of the middle classes. It shows the effects of middle-class values on African-American families.

Macon Dead III alias Milkman is a replica of his class-conscious father. His father, Macon Dead Jr., is a materialist and self-seeking egoist who does not care for others' emotions and feelings. He believes that "Money is freedom" (164). He marries Ruth only because of her money and status. He hates his wife and terrorizes other members of his family. He is so money-oriented that he breaks his relationship with his poor sister, Pilate, and advises his son to steer clear from her: "Let me tell you right now the one important thing you'll ever need to know: own things" (p. 59). Pilate lives in Southside in a narrow single story house with no electricity or gas. She is generally untidy and smelly, and is the town's bootlegger and sings in the streets "like common street women".

Like his father, Milkman sees a woman only as an object. He does not know how to respect a woman. He only pilfers their love and gives nothing in return. As a male chauvinist he abuses the women in his family including his mother, never seeing them as human beings. He is used to being waited upon by them. Milkman becomes an egoist, inconsiderate and insensitive. Women were merely "need providers". As his sister, Magdalena alias Lena, says in anger,

> You've been laughing at us all your life, Corinthians, Mama. Me, using us, ordering us, and judging us: how we cook your food; how we keep your house . . . our girlhood was spent like a found nickle on you. When you slept, we were quite; when you were hungry, we cooked; when you wanted to play, we entertained you; and when you got grown enough to know the difference between a woman and a two-toned Ford, everything in this house stopped for you. . . . And to this day, you have never asked one of us if we were tired, or sad, or wanted a cup of coffee. (p. 215)

Women are treated as objects and possessions. As a result they suppress their feelings and live a parasitical life. There is an antagonistic relationship between men and women in his family. Love is absent. Ryna and Milkman's beloved Hagar both were used as sexpots instead of being perceived as human beings. The narrator comments when Solomon deserts Ryna:

> They say she screamed and screamed, lost her mind completely. You don't hear about women like that anymore, but there used to be more – the kind of woman who couldn't live without a particular man. And when the man left, they lost their minds, or died or something love I guess. (p. 322)

Her cousin, Milkman, also sexually exploits Hagar. She loves him very much: "Totally taken over by her anaconda love, she had no self left, no fears, no wants no intelligence that was her own", while Milkman regarded her as "the third . . . the one you drink because it is there, because it can't hurt, and because what difference does it make"? (p. 94). Hagar is psychologically maimed and deserted by her lover. He has thrown her away "like a wad of chewing gum after the flavour was gone". (p. 277) He is incapable of understanding her deep love. Utterly frustrated and desperate, she makes a futile effort to kill him, but unfortunately she herself dies while longing for her lost love. He used her as "sexual object" rather than as a true companion.

Milkman is so cut-off and isolated from his family that he is the last one to know about the love between his sister Corinthians and Henry Porter. Milkman before leaving Michigan perceives the world in much the same way as his father does. His steadiness of vision and lack of compassion allow him to abuse remorselessly and unconsciously the people around him.

Milkman's father, Macon Dead Jr., is a self-made man orphaned at an early age; he wheels and deals his way as the richest African-American in town. The avid materialism and rugged individualism that makes him financially successful have exacted their price in other ways. Macon has come to believe that property and success are what count in this world. He does little to help the condition of his fellow African-Americans. Macon later recounts to his son, "Negroes in this town worshipped him. He didn't give a damn about them though called them Cannibals". (p. 74) He brutalizes his wife Ruth both subtly and overtly because he suspects her of having incestuous relations with her father and son. He tells his son:

> there's lots of things a man can do to please a woman, even if he can't fuck. Whether or not, the fact is she was in that bed sucking his fingers, and if she do that when he was dead, what'd she do when he was alive? Nothing to do but kill a woman like that. (p. 77)

After the death of her father Ruth has no one with whom she can share:

> She has not had the luxury of blossoming with her mother's milk; her growth is thus artificial, like Pecola's who is forced to drink white milk from a cup. Although she receives love from her father, Ruth appears psychologically damaged and incomplete. She confuses her father's love, much as Pecola confuses Cholly's . . . (Samuels and Hudson, 55)

Her marital life is loveless. She is a sexually frustrated wife. Hence she nurses her son even when he is too old.

Weak Ruth retaliates against her husband's cruelty by manipulating him. Since she cannot attract his attention in any other way, she demeans herself until out of disgust he lashes out at her. Similarly she remarks that her son has never been "a person to her". She feels that there was a bond between herself and Macon, something to hold them together and reinstate their sex. But after the birth of her son, Milkman, she realizes that her husband will never gratify her sexually; she uses Milkman to fulfil her yearning by breast-feeding him until he is old enough to talk.

Macon Dead has aversion for all women but one person he hates more than his wife is his own sister Pilate. Macon says to his son Milkman,

> That woman's (Pilate) no good. She's a snake, and can charm you like a snake, but still a snake. . . . Now I mean for you to stay out of that wine house and as far away from Pilate as you can. (pp. 58-59)

His resentment against Pilate is based in part on his belief that she steals the gold that the two of them should have shared. He fears that the white bankers will cease to trust him if they associate him with a woman bootlegger.

The initiation of Pilate Dead into the rough and tumble of the world takes place during her adolescence. The murder of her father is the first step in that she is on her own after she and Macon separate after a quarrel over a man he has murdered and over gold buried at the murder site. This first experience leaves a great impression on her. The beginning of suffering continues, for she painfully learns that she is not welcome in the African-American community: "I was cut-off from people early. You can't know what that was like" (p. 142). Twice she joins bonds of pickers and get's on well with them until she takes a lover who reports that she has no naval. Taking the lack of navel to be a sign that she is abnormal, the group expels her. Initially she contrives to conceal her belly from her lover, but when he learns that she has no navel, he refuses to marry her. She is cut-off from permanent sexual commitment. After these incidents she has learned the lessons of the world that the African-American world cannot or will not truly accept her. Being strong, she undertakes to build a world of her own, but her place within those boundaries is marginal. She is the bootlegger of the black district, and people come to her house for goods, not for companionship. Her world is both huge and small. Her vision is broad as a result of giving up "all interest table manners or hygiene" and acquiring in its place "a deep concern for and about human relationships" (p. 151). Her father's spirit becomes the source of her wisdom.

In *Song of Solomon* African-Americans are affected by the double consciousness of racial values and gender. Milkman has abandoned every woman in his life, but Pilate alone is the woman who commands his respect and love. Owing to her lack of navel, she is an androgynous figure. She is the one who personifies African-American culture and history. Though Pilate is much like Sula, she is able to do what Sula could not. Unlike her brother she has a deep attachment to nature as she smells "like a forest." She is "the daughter of Nature"; motherless, she is looked after by the forest from her childhood. She, like Eva, is a prototype of the "Great Mother". As William K. Freiert suggests, Pilate's "smooth stomach was a sign that she was not born from human woman - in mystical terms, she is Earth, the Mother of all". (p. 165)

Corianthian Dead, finding herself still a virgin and unemployed at the age of forty-two, becomes conscious of her own self and begins to think of herself. She suffers a severe depression, which lasts until she gets a job as a maid in the house of the poet, Michael Mary Graham. She is also able to find a good life partner, Porter. He is not like other male characters in the novel. All the others like Milkman Dead, Macon Dead and Guitar Bains are heartless and selfish. They only know how to take from others but do not know how to give anything back.

When Milkman breaks off his relationship with Hagar by sending "Thank you" notes on Christmas Eve, she undergoes a traumatic experience, then death because of the utter despair and helplessness. She thinks that Milkman would have loved her if she had possessed perfect physical beauty:

> "He loves Silky hair."
> "Hush, Hagar."
> "Penny - coloured hair."
> "Please, honey."
> "And lemon - coloured skin."
> "Shhh".
> "And gray - blue eyes."
> "Hush now, hush."
> "And thin nose."

"Hush, girl, hush."

"He"s never going to like my hair." (p. 316)

Hagar is very much like Pecola Breedlove. She thinks that her black complexion is the main cause of the broken relationship. Pilate like a prophet tells Hagar not to be the victim of self-negation: "How can he not love your hair? It's the same hair that grows out his crotch on up his stomach". (p. 316)

Milkman's friend Guitar Bains also tells her,

> You think because he doesn't love you that you are worthless. You think because he doesn't want you anymore that he is right – that his judgement and opinion of you are correct. . . . You're turning over your whole life to him. . . . And if it means so little to you that you can just give it away, hand it to him, then why should it mean any more to him? He can't value you more than you value yourself. (pp. 306-7)

Her inability to learn the cause of the broken relationship makes her vindictive, and ultimately she dies frustrated.

So all the women characters, except Pilate, are submissive and enduring. Only Pilate is potent enough to create and realize her individual self. She becomes the spiritual mentor of Milkman. After coming in contact with her, he completely changes and becomes conscious of his identity. She guides him in fulfilling his ambition.

Thus, *Song of Solomon* gives an interesting instance of the manner in which equations of power and the levels of class, gender and race work in a literary work. In order to understand the qualitative leap of Morrison in *Song of Solomon* in regard to the nature of oppression of African-Americans in America and her artistic excellence, her protagonist Milkman's growth can be viewed as having three different but still interconnected developmental stages – the pre-liminal, the liminal and the post-liminal.

Milkman, as his nickname shows, in the pre-liminal stage has a low level of consciousness. As his name suggests, he milks women; this iceberg plays with their love and emotion. Even at thirty-one, he does not know anything about women, and this ignorance is made evident by his inability to differentiate between his sisters and his mother: "Never had he thought of his mother as a person, a separate individual, with a life apart from allowing or interfering with his own" (p. 78). All women characters in this novel give him respect. His mother Ruth, his aunt Pilate, his lover Hagar, and his sisters, Magdalene and Corinthians all give him love, but he is self-centred, heartless and insensitive. He thinks of himself as a king who can do anything and can order everybody around. According to him women are merely need providers. They cater to all sorts of his needs. In exchange for all this, he never shows any consideration and never bothers about their problems.

Although Milkman's search for his individuality is dominant in the entire novel, the focus is on his mother Ruth and his aunt Pilate. Ruth is a society-lady, while Pilate is completely outside of society as symbolized by her house outside of town. Ruth, the only daughter of the African-American doctor in the town, is born and brought up in an upper middle-class family. She is presented in the novel as an ideal southern lady. She is completely cut-off from life and becomes a girl-doll.

While on the one hand, Ruth is the epitome of the ideal southern lady, on the other Pilate is a woman totally outside societal structures. Morrison here compares these two women:

> They were so different, these two women. One black the other lemony. One corseted, the other buck naked under her dress. One well read but ill travelled. The other had read only a geography book, but had been from one end of the country to another. One wholly dependent on money for life, the other indifferent to it. But those were the meaningless things. Their similarities were profound. Both were vitally interested in Macon Dead's son and both had close and supportive posthumous communication with their fathers. (pp. 140-41)

Both of them come together in the novel to protect Milkman who for them is the symbol of their continuity.

Milkman gets plenty of love from Pilate. He feels for "the first time in his life that he remembered being completely happy" (Plakkoottam, p. 85). He learns his first vital lesson in race and class-consciousness from Pilate who, despite her lack of maternal wealth, possesses an innate dignity and takes pride in her African-American tradition: "While she looked as poor as everyone said she was, something was missing from her eyes that should have confirmed it" (p. 42). Under the tutelage of Pilate Milkman begins to realize that money does not ensure happiness. It is she who shows him the right path.

Milkman in the beginning of the novel is confused, he does not know his past, and he is unsure of the future: "Infinite possibilities and enormous responsibilities stretched out before him but he was not prepared to take advantage of the former, or accept the burden of the latter" (p. 71). He lives in limbo, the life of the living dead, always confused whether to go forward or to turn back. Milkman's class-consciousness is just as weak as his race consciousness. Like his father he runs after money. The only motto of his life is to hoard it. He has no respect for the members of his community. Therefore, the people of his community have little regard for him. In order to rise from his present condition, he must learn to love his people like Pilate does and stop hoarding money by whatever means.

Milkman enters the liminal stage of discovery and growth when he beings to question the people and events around him, thereby developing his consciousness. He not only questions "everybody" but also discovers the answers to crucial questions of his identity. What is more, he makes an attempt through his death wish to renounce all that he has learned so far inasmuch as such knowledge brings with it an acceptance of the responsibility of adulthood in general and Africanhood in particular.

Milkman's liminal state, a period of growth though not a full state of consciousness, can be documented by his increasing awareness of race and class. His awareness of race is made more poignant by his personal confrontation with the police. Stripped of his dignity, emasculated like millions of other African men throughout the world, he is filled with shame:

> Shame at being spread-eagled, fingered, and handcuffed. . . . But nothing was like the shame he felt as he watched and listened to Pilate. Not just her Aunt Jemica act, but the fact that she was both adept at it and willing to do it - for him. (pp. 210-11)

While he feels ashamed of his father who buckles before the policemen, Milkman is proud of Pilate who sacrifices her dignity to free him from jail even when he was prepared to knock her down if she had come into the room while he was stealing from her. The fact that Milkman finds more dignity and life in poor Pilate than in rich Mecon increases his class-consciousness.

The incident with the police is the second that contributes to Milkman's developing class-consciousness. The first results from the appearance of the white peacock, symbolizing both the race and wealth of the ruling class in the United States. Ironically the peacock appears while Guitar and Milkman are planning to rob Pilate's gold. Significantly, it is Milkman who first sees it, "poised on the roof of a long low building that served as headquarters for Nelson Buick" (p. 179). Equating both flight and money with freedom, Milkman asks Guitar why a peacock cannot fly. Although Milkman is not yet fully conscious of the connection between the diamond - like tail of the peacock and the gold he is planning to steal from Pilate, it will only impede his quest for self. This incident contributes a great deal to his growing class-consciousness.

His initiation into a new society, the society of the Shalimar hunters, characterizes Milkman's post-liminal stage, which marks the height of his awareness. According to Arnold Van Gennep, one must undergo several initiation rites prior to being incorporated into a new society. Milkman, after coming into the new society, accepts his responsibility of adulthood and Africanhood for "he had stopped evading things, sliding through, over, and around difficulties" (p. 271). He now starts giving respect to the natural world rather than the material world; he becomes a more balanced person:

> There was nothing here [on the Shalimar hunt] to help him – not his money, his car, his father's reputation, his suit or his shoes. In fact they hampered him. . . . They [the hunters] hooted and laughed all the way back to the car, teasing Milkman, egging him on to tell more about how scared he was. And he told them. Laughing too, hard, loud and long. Really laughing. (pp. 277-80)

So far as race is concerned, Milkman's higher level of awareness is exemplified on the two occasions when he comes to know about his grandfather's assassination and takes part in the Shalimar hunt. When Milkman first learns of his grandfather's murder from Pilate, he is more or less oblivious to race, but when he hears of the murder a second time, he becomes angry and asks why the Danville Africans did not seek revenge: "And nobody did anything? Milkman wondered at his own anger, he hadn't felt angry when he first heard about it. Why now?" (Mbalia, p. 59). On this occasion he is infuriated, because of his heightened awareness of himself and other African-American folk. Ultimately his consciousness manifests itself in a devoted love for his own people.

Milkman's class-consciousness is also heightened during the Shalimar hunt. Now he starts respecting and loving his people and tradition like Pilate, who plants the seed of humanism in him.

As far as gender is concerned, it is only after developing race and class-consciousness that Milkman is able to overcome his patriarchal attitude. Pissing on Lena, squealing on First Corinthians, spying on Ruth, stealing from Pilate, and killing his lover, Hagar are examples of his low level of consciousness. Now after being in touch with Pilate he is able to see women as his equals and tries to understand the reciprocal nature of human relationships. Like his father, he has never bothered to cherish human relationships. Butnow his name "Milkman" signifies a more positive meaning. He becomes the Milkman who is able to act as a source of life for those who are in need. At last he sheds his father's materialism and accepts Pilate's humanism.

Milkman's developed consciousness is grounded in his journey to the south, a journey which opens his eyes and his mind:

> With two exceptions, everybody he was close to seemed to prefer him out of this life. And the two exceptions were both women, both black, both old. From the beginning, his mother and Pilate had fought for his life, and he had never so much as made either of a cup of tea. (p. 329)

He gives credit of his growth as a man to Hagar's sacrificial death and Pilate's far-seeing wisdom. This admission of his weakness is a significant step toward recovery and knowledge. He then starts to respect the poor African-Americans around him, as well as all the helpful women. Now he is able to understand the significance of life, its shallowness, artificiality and false values. The Shalimar journey makes him realize how his past life was empty and meaningless. At the end of novel, we see a new Milkman whose physical and geographical journey has enabled him to grow spiritually and emotionally. He is a changed person, a man who repents for his past sins. Pilate dies, but he embraces her mantle of honesty, humanity, wisdom and clear sightedness. Thus, Milkman discovers that there is hope for the future and that Pilate's prophecy comes true: "He don't know what he loves, but he'll come around one of these days". (p. 55)

Thus, realizing that to overcome his crisis he must first understand how he became crisis-ridden, thereby knowing his history, Milkman comes to understand how operates at the levels of class, race and gender and, what is more, learns to identify himself with the African masses and not, like Sula, to distinguish himself from them. However, it is important to remember that such a realization and identification are not enough. Milkman must understand that his awareness of the common oppression of African people as manifested in their history and in their present is relevant only if it is used to struggle against the cause of that oppression. Unfortunately Milkman sees himself as an African-American exploited by capitalism and oppressed by racism but offers no solution to this dilemma. While his race and class-consciousness develop sufficiently to allow him to recreate self, it never reaches the point where he moves beyond self-healing to other-healing.

Song of Solomon shows the effects of middle-class values on African-American families. Like Alex Haley's *Roots*, it illustrates the importance of African awareness and acceptance of their history in order to liberate themselves from oppression. Though Milkman's quest for self is the dominant thread of the novel, the major obstacle he has to overcome is the deadening effect of capitalism. He is accidentally propelled into a search for a self as a result of his desire for gold. The long journey leads him back through his personal past to his racial history. His knowledge liberates him, and he begins to respect the poor African-Americans around him as well as the sweet women, Pilate and Hagar, who have constantly helped him.

4

Tar Baby: The Cultural Schism in the Self

The truth about African-American identity gets problematized even further in Morrison's fourth novel, *Tar Baby,* which gives voice to much that is left unspoken in the previous novels. Unlike her earlier novels, in *Tar Baby* she places these issues of race, gender and class in a contemporary context and does not associate them with an earlier time and place. It also exposes all the conflicts that result from cultural encounter between the colonizers and colonized.

This is the first of Morrison's novels with White people as central characters. This novel is free from the narrow geographical boundaries of the U.S.A. It is set on a Caribbean Island, the Isle des Chevaliers, the home of a retired American candy mogul, Valerian Street.

By setting her fiction in the Caribbean, Morrison wants to include many different cultures including the island natives, Philadelphia African-Americans, and Western imperialists who are mutually dependent on one another to fulfil their financial needs but at the same time are separated from any sense of community. The geographical background of characters plays a significant role inasmuch as land and communities are part of the African-American heritage. Barbara Christian observes:

> As in the ancestral African tradition place is as important as the human actors. For the land is a participant in the maintenance of folk tradition. It is one of the necessary constants through which the folk dramatize the meaning of life, as it is passed on from one generation to the next. Setting then is organic to the characters' view of themselves. And a change in place drastically alters the traditional values that give their life coherence. (p. 65)

In *Tar Baby* Morrison's focus is on class struggle, the struggle between the ruling class and the subject class. Her awareness is reflected in her ability to seek connections between class, race and sex.

Morrison describes the tragic consequences for African-American people when they blindly follow and embrace the ideals of White society. Racial discrimination emanates not only from the White but also the African-American society. For instance, the African-American community condemns Pecola and Hager because they are ugly by White standards of beauty. Consequently they themselves hate their black skin. Both die at last, one mentally, the other physically. Here Jadine, the protagonist, dies culturally and spiritually because she mimics White values and is alienated from her native culture. In this novel Whites do not hate African-Americans, but African-Americans hate African-Americans. Jadine feels that she is not an African-American but a Euro-American. She is a modern woman who has no respect for the culture and norms of African-American people. At a very early age she loses her father and mother and is adopted by her uncle Sydney and her aunt Ondine. As Sydney and Ondine work for the White family of Valerian and Margaret Street, she is raised under the care and protection of the Streets. As a result she loses touch with both the worlds, African-American as well as White. She desires money and fame. Coleman correctly calls her "an antithesis of the black folk and community values". (p. 64) She gets lured by glitter and glamour and considers her aunt as backward. Ondine teaches her the idea of woman:

> Jadine, a girl has to be a daughter first, she have to learn that. And if she never learns how to be a daughter. She can't never learn how to be a woman. I mean a real woman: a woman good enough for a child; good enough for a man—good enough even for the respect of other women. (p. 283)

She objects immediately:

> "There are other ways to be a woman, Nandine", Jadine went on. "Your way is one, I guess it is, but it's not my way. I don't want to be . . . like you. . . . I don't want to be that kind of woman". (p. 284)

Morrison's most intricate exploration of the African petty bourgeois is expressed through Jadine. She is oblivious of her origin and roots. In her remembrance of her engagement with the Frenchman she broods:

> I wonder if the person he wants to marry is me or a black girl? And if it isn't me he wants, but any black girl who looks like me, talks and acts like me, what will happen when he finds out that I hate ear hoops, that I don't have to straighten my hair, that Mingus puts me to sleep, that sometimes I want to get out of my skin and be only the person inside — not American — not black—Just me? (p. 45)

The folklore of the tar baby serves as a motif in this novel. It takes its point of departure from the old folk tale of Br'er Rabbit:

> A farmer sets out a tar baby dressed in bonnet and skirt to trap a troublesome rabbit. The rabbit hits the tar baby when it does not answer good morning. He gets stuck and when caught he begs the farmer, "boil me in oil, skin me alive but please don't throw me in the briar patch". The farmer falls for the trick. So he throws him in the briar patch and the clever rabbit escapes. (Leclair, p. 27)

In the context of this folktale, Jadine Childs is the tar

baby who traps Son, the African-American man who stands for the Afro-centric values but falls prey to the White materialistic values that she represents. In addition to this, Morrison also suggests another meaning for tar baby:

> I found that there is a tar baby in American mythology I started thinking about her. At one time a tar pit was a holy place, at last important because tar was used to build things. . . . It held things together. For, the tar baby goes comes to mean the black woman who can hold things together. (Leclair, p. 122)

This is the quality of tar—to hold things together—that Jadine is missing, and as a result she acts as a tar baby created by farmer Valerian to catch a rabbit, Son, who is the bearer of the African-American culture and values.

Later Morrison adds another story of the Ant Kingdom in the novel. Its moral suggests that neither dreaming nor security is obtainable for women. In the beginning she explains that women are the embodiment of security themselves. Moreover, life places such needs on them that they simply do not have the time for anything else. The legend of the soldier ants, most of whom are women, makes this implication explicit. The nature of the relation between male and female ants parallels that between Jadine and Son. According to Theàese, Son is like a descendent of the island's mythical blind equestrian. His motto is to set her free in the way these warriors set free many African-Americans on the island. "I told you! said Theàese. He's a horseman come down here to get her". (p. 107) Josie Campbell gives his views: Jadine "is able to feel unorphaned when Son tries to reorient her culturally toward the values of her own race". (p. 402)

Once Jadine makes a decision that she cannot be a culture bearer like Son, she terminates her relationship with him and goes back to embrace the world of glitter and glamour. Just as a male ant dies, similarly Son dies emotionally after Jadine's abandonment:

> this little Amazon trembled in the air waiting for a male to mount her . . . frenzied, he fills into the

> humming cloud to fight gravity and time in order to do, just once, the single thing he was born for. Then he drops dead, having emptied his sperm into his lady-love. (p. 293)

Like the "little Amazon" Jadine, too is "airborne, suspended, open, trusting, frightened, determined, vulnerable—girlish. . . ." (p. 294)

As the class struggle is the dominant theme in the novel, it is necessary to analyse the novel from this point of view. Valerian Street, a White man, is a representative of capitalistic society. He is a person who runs after money and has made his fortune by exploiting the labour of poor African-American people and by taking their land. And it is quite important that

> his wealth emanates from the production of candy, the main ingredients of which—sugar and cocoa—come from the Caribbean, once the sugar capital of the Western world. (Williams, p. 28)

He insults Gideon and Therese for stealing a couple of apples. It shows his inhumanity towards African-American people. He is named after a plant, the dried root of which has small clusters of white or pinkish flowers used medicinally as a sedative; he is asleep throughout most of his adult life. He is always unconcerned about his workers, which is why Ondine shouts, "I may be cook, Mr. Street, but I am a person too" (p. 208). Valerian measures a person's worth by the wealth that he owns. He wishes to control other people's lives; he spends his money in order to impress others. For instance he buys expensive dresses for Margaret and bears Jadine's college expenses.

Valerian, Sydney, Ondine and Jadine mimic the behavioural patterns, dress, and language of their White masters. Ondine and Sydney feel privileged to be the servants of such important and rich masters. Ondine calls the Streets' kitchen "my kitchen" and adopts her master's culture as her own. Perhaps according to their surname Childes, they are indeed the children of Valerian who do as they are ordered. Sydney proudly reveals his ignorance of African culture:

> I am a Phil-a-delphia Negro mentioned in the book of the very same name. My people owned drugstores and taught school while yours were still cutting their faces open so as to be able to tell one of you from the other. (p. 164)

However, Morrison's most intricate exploration of the African petty bourgeois is expressed through Jadine, not through Sydney and Ondine. Jadine is a Europeanized African and an art graduate. She loses her identity, internalizes the White values to such an extent that she apes their pattern of dress, language, association and ideology and despises the African-American norm and heritage. Not only does she think like a European, but she feels that she is a European. When she finds Son in her closet, she thinks that since he is an African-American man, he will rape her. Son's response is very revealing: "Rape? Why you little White girls always think somebody's trying to rape you?" (p. 121). Contrary to Jadine, Mr. Street protects Son and tries to help him. Jadine thinks that Mr. Street is mistaken: "I know you're an animal because I smell you" (p. 122).

Jadine often thinks of herself as an adoring daughter of the Streets. She keeps herself away from African-American values and is ashamed of her heritage. Michael, Valerian's son, wants to politicize her Africanness:

> Actually we didn't talk; we quarrelled. About why I was studying art history at that snotty school instead of – I don't know what. Organizing or something. He said I was abandoning my history. My people. (pp. 70-71)

Thus, by neglecting the history of her race she rejects her real self, and in place of it, she tries to transplant the White "self". Though Sydney and Ondine are all the family she has, Valerian provides everything for her. Jadine never understands that Valerian has been taking care of her because her uncle Sydney and aunt Ondine have been working for the Streets all their lives. However, all the education that she receives does not tell her anything about her own people and her history. Thus Jadine is trained, educated and brainwashed to ignore her own history and culture.

Jadine has so absorbed capitalist values that she considers Son primitive, backward and uncivilized in the initial stage of her relationship and also in the final stage when she gets an opportunity to live with him in Eloe, Son's birthplace. The very presence of Son in L'Arbede La Croix, the home of the Streets, is repulsive to her in the beginning but later on changes into a fascination with him. As a result, she falls in love with blackness. Son's very presence restores something of her African-American awareness and forces her to recall the guilt she had felt two months ago when a beautiful African woman in a canary yellow dress spit on her in disgust in a Paris street:

> The skin like tar against the canary yellow dress? The woman walked down the aisle as though her many-coloured sandals were pressing gold tracks on the floor. . . .
>
> Jadine followed her profile, then her back as she passed the store window . . . the woman turned her head sharply around the left and looked right at Jadine. Turned those eyes too beautiful for eyelashes on Jadine and, with a small parting of her lips, shot an arrow of saliva between her teeth down to the pavement and the hearts below. (pp. 42-43)

Jadine is haunted by the thought of the woman and the look in her eyes as she spat at her. That

> "arrow of saliva" is clearly a sign of the African woman's disdain for Jadine and what she represents, yet, she couldn't figure out why the woman's insulting gesture had derailed her, shaken her out of proportion to incident. Why she had wanted that women to like and respect her. (Harvard and Irving, p. 51)

Barbara Christian comments on Morrison's purpose in presenting the woman in the yellow dress:

> that Morrison uses the image of the African woman in yellow dress as a symbol for the authenticity that the jaded Jadine lacks. It is this woman's inner strength, beauty and pride manifested in the defiant stance of her body, that haunts Jadine's dream and throws her into such a state of confusion - cultural confusion. ("Trajectories of the Self Definitions", p. 244)

The woman in yellow makes us remember about the navelless Pilate in *Song of Solomon*. As the Paris vision holds the eggs aloft, one remembers Pilate's giving of eggs and apples to Milkman as he learns with Pilate to respect African values. In both novels eggs suggest origins and encourage a return to the past.

After this incident Jadine begins questioning her life and its direction. She travels to the island to be with her relatives and benefactor in order to think and sort out her confusion. Thus her encounter with the "woman in yellow" causes her to realize that her acceptance of Western values has denied her the potential for exploring and realizing her own history and culture. She is made to evaluate herself on the basis of a visual exchange and gesture that offer an external definition of self by the "other".

However, once she accepts Son, she moves away from her Whiteness to meet the genuine authenticity of blackness represented by Son and his world. In his company Jadine temporarily finds something that is restorative in his impulsiveness and powerful African-American pride. When Son takes her to his lost garden in Eloe, it is apparent that she can't live in his world of poverty, ignorance and isolation. Eloe, in fact, embodies all the "blackness" she had long struggled to escape.

Yet their trip to Eloe is very important. It is here on the island that she learns about authentic blackness and love. After this trip with Son, Jadine begins to confront her own inner ambiguities and tensions. On one occasion, for instance, she walks into the forest in order to get out of the swamp and suddenly finds herself sinking in a quagmire. Mud covers her from her waist down and threatens to pull her in deeper. The image is that of a woman cut in half, half of her covered with blackness, the other half white. Jadine is so far away from her community that she becomes a part of the West. The familiar world at Eloe is shockingly new to her, and she is unable to become one with African-American people. In Eloe, Jadine for the first time realizes her nudity when aunt Rosa accidentally finds her naked in bed. She reflects, "No man had made her feel that naked, that unclothed. Leerers, lovers, doctors, artists – none of them had made her feel exposed. More than exposed. Obscene." (p. 255)

On the island Jadine is exposed for the first time to various dimensions of African-American selfhood. An almost overwhelming and recurring image that seems to occupy her imagination is that of big-breasted women. While most men have looked upon Jadine purely as an object of lust, these women offer her a vision of different kind. Jadine is taught by them the principle of nurture and the significance of one's own African-American womanhood. In a waking nightmare she comes across African-American women who expose their breasts in defiance. The women in her dream have not forgotten their ancient properties. Jadine, however, wants to be a new type of African-American woman, a woman whose life is not based on traditional experience.

Jadine is not the victim of gender oppression. She is an independent successful model. But she is doubly orphaned as has been pointed out by Samuels and Hudson in "Folklore as Matrix for cultural Affirmation in *Tar Baby*":

> Jadine's status as an orphan is significant, for it may be ascribed to her in diverse ways. At the crucial age of twelve, a point of transition from childhood to adolescence, she is deprived of parents to nurture and guide her. There is no Pilate in her life, unlike Pilate, who passes the legacy of her cultural heritage

> of her nephew, Milkman, Ondine does not perform this function for Jadine. (p. 83)

This sophisticated art-graduate model is "the epitome of ideal white womanhood" (Heinze, p. 87).

Unlike Jadine, Son is race-conscious and a lover of his native land. He is "a human being capable of spiritual, emotional and intellectual growth" (Heinze, p. 90). He embodies African-American values, whereas Jadine embodies White values. Like a Christ figure on L'Arbe des La Croix, he saves his people. He loves to be in a natural environment and, as a consequence, is attuned to nature. Unlike Jadine, Sydney and Ondine, who have no love and emotion for struggling African people, he has that sensitiveness. For instance, he looks at Gideon and compares the yardman with himself:

> Yardman - he was kneeling, chopping at the trunk of a small tree - while he himself was so spanking clean, clean from the roots of his hair to the crevices between his toes . . . now he was as near to crying as he'd been since he'd fled from home. . . . "Thanks," whispered Son. (p. 140)

He sees himself as a member of the exploited class, although he himself is not exploited. He is the only one who changes Jadine to some extent, but that change is very little. She thinks that she cannot adapt to his world, and Son too feels the same way: "Jadine, saturated with (jaded by) Western culture, maintains a more linear perspective. While Son, the progeny of African culture, maintains a more cyclical one" (Samuels and Hudson, p. 85).

When Jadine insists on Son getting a law degree so that both can be employed and educated, he protests, "I don't want to know their [white] laws; I want to know mine" (p. 265), and he comments on Jadine's apathetic attitude: "what the hell kind of education is it that didn't teach you about Gideon and Old Man and me. Nothing about me!" (p. 267).

Son does attempt to disabuse Jadine of her capitalist ideology, but that change is momentary. She resists any efforts on his part to sensitize her to the life of African-American people. Any hope that she is undergoing an ideological renaissance is rendered false in the light of her response to being back in New York: "This is home, she thought with an orphan's delight; not Paris, not Baltimore, not Philadelphia. This is home" (p. 223). Obviously Jadine is referring to petty bourgeois African-American women like herself, because for an ordinary African-American woman New York is nothing more than hell. It is, in fact, symbolic of the capitalist world, reflecting the two extremes of capitalist: the poor struggling African-American people and the affluent European finance bankers and corporate magnates.

As Jadine loves New York and sees it as her home, it is not surprising that she hates Son's Eden, Eloe, which is just the opposite of New York. When Jadine goes to Eloe, she behaves like a typical European tourist: she takes photographs of poor people, laughs at them and insults them. Moreover, because she has a longer association with Europeans than with Africans, her ways are, in fact, more European than African. Figuratively and literally, Eloe is the blackest thing she has ever seen: "she might as well have been a cave, a grave, the dark womb of earth, suffocating" (p. 217). It is, indeed too black, too much like Africa and its culture for Jadine. Thus, her willingness to share her life with Son, an African man attuned to his culture, becomes contingent upon his willingness to embrace the capitalist ideology that she holds so dear.

Geographical, cultural and economic disparities destroy their relationship. Jadine loves New York, and Son loves his native land Eloe. She forgets that she is also part and parcel of the same race. After coming from Florida, Son's home, she goes back to her sophisticated world of fashion. For her Eloe is the worst place. When she finds that Son cannot be changed, she says,

> I can't let you hurt me again. You stay in that medieval slave basket if you want to. You will stay there by yourself. Don't ask me to do it with you. I won't. There is nothing any of us can do about the past but

> make our own lives better, that's all I've been trying to help you do. That is the only revenge, for us to get over. Way over. (p. 274)

Both are incapable of accepting each other's values. Jadine cannot accept the African-American past, and Son cannot accept her White present. Morrison has correctly evaluated their situations: "Both are inadequate positions today, unless you are very sure. She [Jadine] hasn't enough of what he has and he [Son] doesn't have enough of what she has" (qtd. in Samuels & Hudson, p. 87).

As their interests and attitudes are diametrically opposed, their relationship can only endure if one of them is ready to change. As a result, their relationship collapses. Instead of going back to woebegone days, Son and Jadine, in particular, and all African-American people, in general, must extract the positive things from traditional Africa and modern capitalism, with Africa as the center in order to forge a new society.

Morrison in this novel depicts the most compelling relationship between class and race. Jadine is presented as class-bound while Son is race bound. Jadine mimics not only Whites but wants to be an upper-class White. She is not like the ideal Southern White lady who depends on her husband's money and status. She wants equality, but it must be equality in the world of materialism. She is a very selfish person who is not concerned about anyone, not even about her aunt and uncle, who make her access to wealth possible by becoming life-long servants to the affluent Valerian Street. She is a feminist without any concern for social justice.

In contrast to Jadine, Son is proud to be an African. Like Pilate in *Song of Solomon,* he resists the material world of gain. Still, he has not any future as Pilate has, for he really lives in Eloe, a poor community.

Both Son and Jadine are at a dead end since things do not resolve in their favour. Jadine returns to her former lifestyle in Paris, whereas Son returns to his roots. Morrison in the end clearly shows what the possibilities are for Son, a twentieth-century African-American man burdened with African norms and customs, and for Jadine, a twentieth-century African-American woman who reverts to Westernization.

Morrison has conveyed in this novel the importance of the spiritual and the physical worlds that both contradict and complement each other. In their search for selfhood, Morrison points out, there are boundless levels of existence to be experienced in the physical and spiritual worlds. In fact, their traditional limited concepts of life prove to have little impact upon many of their experiences, such as the unexpected encounter with mysticism.

Tar Baby, like other Morrison novels, reveals the failed relationship between an African-American man and an African-American woman. In this novel, unlike previous ones, it is the woman who leaves the man, Jadine who leaves Son. When Son and Jadine fight, she like a Virago "kept barking at him about equality, sexual equality, as though he thought women were inferiors" (270). This altercation shows how bold and courageous she is! This conflict of gender comes from a "cultural illness". Son's effort to "insert" a cultural awareness into Jadine and Jadine's attempt to "press" her capitalist wish onto Son reflect the gendered aspects of this dispute. As J.S. Ryan states, "Son's and Jadine's competing agendas for rescue and conflicting perceptions of the threat facing them underscore the cultural thematic axis in the novel". (p. 602)

When Jadine rejects Son for Paris he becomes "mad" to some extent. Jadine, on the other hand, is relaxed and at ease: "Aboard the 707 Jadine had free use of the seat next to her. . . . No more dreams of safety". (p. 292) When a woman leaves a man, his male pride is hurt, and he becomes restless. That is why Son "cannot live without her. The tar baby and the rabbit lock in a fatal embrace" (Strouse, p. 57).

Tar Baby dramatizes a pronounced crisis in cross-generational interactions. Jadine achieves an independence not attained by Sula, but Morrison concentrates on the cost and negative aspects of her achievement. The ultimate horror of bourgeois society that Morrison explores results in both alienation and repression. None of Morrison's African-American characters actually ascends to the upper reaches of bourgeois rehabilitation, but there are some who come close. They are saved only because they remain marginal to the bourgeois class and are imperfectly assimilated to bourgeois values.

In her novels what emerges about slavery is that both groups usually see themselves as bound to each other by their race, culture and oppression. Morrison also uses another aspect of the old stereotypes by characterizing the house slave as female and the field slave as male, an assertion that is also negated by history. Yet, if Morrison's perceptions are correct, the tremendous effects of American values on African-Americans in this century may mean that we are worse off than we were a hundred years ago.

Tar Baby raises the question all African-Americans must ask themselves: Do I identify with my oppression or my people? And its ending provides an answer. Unfortunately, however, Morrison does not provide a viable alternative existence for African-American people.

5

Beloved: Unshackling History

Morrison's award winning novel, *Beloved* deals with the story of an African-American female slave, Sethe, who takes her daughter's life to save her from the shackles of slavery. It is a novel about slavery and about the history of race-based oppression. It not only unveils that "peculiar phase of slavery" which "has generally been kept veiled" (Puri 156), i.e., the tale of sexual abuse, but also critically comments on the inequities that African-American women still face. Indeed, all of Morrison's novels have been constructed and are unsettled by the unique character of the historical memory for African–Americans. With each of her earlier novels, Morrison was inching her way back beyond the twentieth-century experiencing of racism, poverty and injustice towards its origins in the history of slavery. She got the idea of this novel when as an editor at Random House, she was thumbing througl news article entitled "A Visit to the Slave Mother who Killed her Child". She decided to write a novel on this theme, since it stirred her heart and mind:

> I found her with an infant in her arms only a few months old, and observed that it had a large bunch on its forehead. I inquired the cause of the injury. She then proceeded to give a detailed account of her attempt to kill her children.

She said, that when the officers and slave-hunters came to the house in which they were concealed, she caught a shovel and struck two of her children on the head, and then took a knife and cut the throat of the third, and tried to kill the other—that if they had given her time, she would have killed them all—that with regard to herself, she cared but little, but she was unwilling to have her children suffer as she had done.

When inquired if she was not excited almost to madness when she committed the act. No, she replied, I was as cool as I am now; and would much rather kill them at once, and thus end their sufferings, than have them taken back to slavery, and be murdered by the piecemeal. She then told the story of her wrongs. She spoke of her days of suffering, of her nights of unmitigated toil, while the bitter tears coursed their way down her cheeks and fell in the face of the innocent child as it looked smiling up, little conscious of the danger and probable suffering that awaited it. . . .

The two men and the two other children were in another apartment but her mother-in-law was in the same room. She says she is the mother of eight children, most of whom have been separated from her; that her husband was once separated from her twenty-five years, during which time she did not see him; that could she have prevented it, she would never have permitted him to return, as she did not wish him to witness her sufferings, or be exposed to the brutal treatment that he would receive.

She states that she has been a faithful servant, and in her old age she would not have attempted to obtain her liberty; but as she became feeble, and less capable of performing labour, her master became more and more exacting and brutal in his treatment,

> until she could stand it no longer; that the effort could result only in death, at most, she therefore made the attempt.
>
> She witnessed the killing of the child, but said she neither encouraged nor discouraged her daughter-in-law – for under similar circumstances she should probably have done the same. The old woman is from sixty to seventy years of age, has been a professor of religion about twenty years, and speaks with much feeling of the time when she shall be delivered from the power of the oppressor, and dwell with the saviour, "where the wicked cease from troubling, and the weary are at rest".
>
> These slaves (as far as I am informed) have resided all their lives within sixteen miles of Cincinnati. We are frequently told that Kentucky slavery is very innocent. If these are its fruits, where it exists in a mild form, will some one tell us what we may expect from its more objectionable features? But comments are unnecessary. (Bassett, p. 29)

Beloved is the story of Sethe's quest for social freedom and psychological wholeness. She struggles with the haunting memory of her slavery and the retribution of Beloved, the ghost of her dead daughter whom she has murdered in order to protect her from the living death of slavery. The entire novel hinges on the death of Beloved who mysteriously comes back as a sensuous young woman in order to claim her mother's love. So *Beloved* is an amalgamation of the past and present experiences of an escaped female slave. It is set in post-Civil War Ohio on the edge of Cincinnati. It begins in 1873, with Sethe and her adolescent daughter Denver living alone in house number 124 Bluestone Road, a house haunted by a dead baby. She is the centre of the novel. It also deals with her former life as a slave at sweet Home Farm. She comes to Sweet Home at the age of thirteen, which is neither Sweet nor Home, to replace old Baby Suggs who is sixty years old and has given birth to eight children by six fathers. Morrison narrates Sethe's appearance on the Plantation as follows:

> Sethe was thirteen when she came to Sweet Home and already iron-eyed. She was a timely present for Mrs. Garner who had lost Baby Suggs to her husband's high principles. The five Sweet Home men looked at the new girl decided to let her be. They were young and so sick with the absence of woman they had taken to calves. Yet they let the iron-eyed girl be, so she could choose in spite of the fact that each one would have beaten the others to mush to have her. . . . The restraint they had exercised possible only because they were Sweet Home men – the ones Mr. Garner bragged about while other farmers shook their heads in warning at the phrase. (p. 10)

After two years of her arrival at Sweet Home, Sethe gets married to Halle and gives birth to four children, Howard, Buglar, Denver and Beloved. She thinks of Sweet Home as her real home. But the atmosphere there becomes intolerable after the death of Mr. Garner. Since Mrs. Garner is the only White woman on the Plantation with six African-American male slaves, her brother-in-law, a schoolteacher, comes to Sweet Home to help her. After that Sethe is forced to face the atrocities and brutalities of slavery. Now she realizes that Sweet Home is "a wonderful lie". When Sethe overhears the secret discussion between the schoolteacher and his nephew, she is shocked. He asks his nephew to "put her [Sethe's] human characteristics on the left; her animal ones on the right". (p. 193) His intention is to sell her children when they grow up.

So Sethe decides to run away from the plantation and arrives at 124 Bluestone Road, Cincinnati. What Sethe plans for the children is safety and security but after reaching Cincinnati, she realizes that slave masters are very powerful, and it is not easy to keep her children out of their reach. She is in a dilemma and does not want to see her children condemned to slavery:

> I couldn't let all that go back to where it was, and I couldn't let her nor any of them live under schoolteacher. That was out . . . . She was squatting in the garden and when she saw them coming and recognized schoolteacher's hat, she heard wings. Little hummingbirds stuck their needle beaks right through her headcloth into her hair and beat their wings. And if she thought anything, it was No. No. None. Nonono simple. She just flew. Collected every bit of life she had made, all the parts of her that were precious and fine and beautiful and carried, pushed, dragged them through the veil, out, away over there where no one could hurt them. Over there, outside this place; where they would be safe. (p. 163)

She is therefore determined not to send her children back into slavery; she places her children in "safety with a handsaw" (p. 164) and feels more secure after committing this act.

In spite of committing this crime Sethe does not feel any remorse. Like Eva in *Sula* who defends herself when Hannah asks her the purpose of killing Plum, Sethe too argues with Paul D. and shows no regret:

> "Yeah. It didn't work, did it? Did it work?" he asked
>
> "It worked," she said.
>
> "How? Your boys gone you don't know where. One girl dead, the other won't leave the yard. How did it work?"
>
> "They ain't at Sweet Home. Schoolteacher ain't got'em."
>
> "May be there's worse."
>
> "It ain't my job to know what's worse. It's my job to know what is and to keep them away from what I know is terrible. I did that."

"What you did was wrong, Sethe". (p. 164-165)

She considers it a "mercy-killing." Sethe's infanticide becomes her act of maternal love. According to her, death is better than slavery, and it is necessary for her protection and self-esteem: "Sethe did what was right although she did not have the right to do it" (qtd. in Samuels & Hudson, p. 111). And Sethe "like Dubois, sees death as a Sanctuary from an oppressive life. . . . The act of murder was not perceived as a senseless crime but as a necessity". (Samuels & Hudson, p. 106)

Sethe further asserts that it is obligatory for a mother to give her children safety and protection, "even if it means prostituting herself like the 'Saturday girls' who sell their bodies in the slaughter house Yard". (p. 106) So she does not feel sorry for it. She would never have committed this crime if the system allowed her and her family to live with dignity. Her efforts to save her children from slavery are presented through bird imagery: "Sethe heard wings. Little hummingbirds stuck their needle beaks right through her headcloth into her hair and beat their wings. . . . She just flew" (p. 163). And again when she thinks that the grown Beloved is in danger, "she hears wings. Little hummingbirds stick needle beaks right through her headcloth into her hair are beat their wings. And if she thinks any thing, it is no. No no. Nonono. She flies" (p. 262).

The ordeal of Sethe's sexual oppression is so traumatic to that she does not hesitate to commit a crime. Killing her daughter could not kill her maternal love, but she is haunted by the spectre of the baby she has killed. Beloved's reincarnation brings back several of Sethe's painful repressed memories of her enslaved past, which she and her community would like to forget. At the end of the novel, Beloved seems to disappear and the community forgets her "like a bad dream" (274). Sethe takes this decision of killing her daughter because she herself has been psychologically and physically maimed and violated several times because she is both black and female.

She, like Morrison's other female characters, is a victim of both sexist and racist oppression. Sethe is a runaway slave, a slave mother, who is brutally treated by White men, the schoolteacher and his nephews. How can she forget the humiliation of her nurturing abilities as a mother, the stealing of her milk? She shares her experience with Paul D. : "After I left you, those boys came in there and took my milk. That's what they came in there for. Held me down and took it" (p. 16).

Sethe repeatedly asserts that like a cow her slave masters milked her, so she feels robbed of her essence. We also come to know that as a child, Sethe was deprived of her own mother's milk. "There was no nursing milk to call my own. I know what it is to be without the milk that belongs to you". (p. 200) Thus she is ravaged as an infant and robbed of her essence by the system of slavery. This situation has severely wounded her.

In *Beloved* sexual assault is not a visible problem that exists between African men and women but is one that exists within the context of the economic relation between master and slave and race is only a later justification of the oppression of African-American people. The rapport between African-American men and women is not antagonistic. It is positive.

Paul D. is the Son of *Tar Baby* who comes back to the struggle, wiser and more committed. He is a gentleman who has never mistreated a woman in his entire life, and as a man he is grateful to women for giving him life. He is Christ-like on some occasions, at least in his manner toward women: "There was something blessed in his manner. Women saw him and wanted to weep - to tell him that their chest hurt and their knees did too" (p. 17). The moment he sees Sethe after several years, "He rubbed his cheek on her back and learned that way for sorrow, the roots of it; its wide trunk and intricate branches" (p. 17). It is his presence at 124 Bluestone that forces the essential purgative interaction between Sethe, the community, and Beloved. Indeed Paul D. is the only major male character in the Morrison canon who has positive relations with a woman and, furthermore, who fights with a woman to forge this positive relationship. He believes that "only this woman Sethe could have left him his manhood like that. He wants to put his story next to hers". (p. 273)

It is a mark of Toni Morrison's heightened consciousness that she depicts the life that Paul D. struggles to build with Sethe as one based on a common history and a common struggle. It is not based just on sex like the Milkman-Sweet affair in *Song of Solomon,* nor on physical appearance like the Son-Jadine affair in *Tar Baby*. Sethe is a typical African-American woman who is satisfied with the real happiness love brings, not with the artificial contentment brought by status and wealth:

> Perhaps, it was the smile, or maybe the ever-ready love she saw in his eyes—easy and upfront, the way colts, evangelists and children look at you: with love you don't have to deserve—that made her go ahead and tell him what she had not told Baby Suggs, the only person she felt obliged to explain anything to. (p. 161)

Unlike Son and Jadine, Paul D. and Sethe fight together in order to make a positive life under the most adverse circumstances.

Class oppression is not overtly and clearly presented in this novel, but a close examination reveals that gender and race violence is the result of the exploitative economic system. Eric William observes in *Capitalism and Slavery* (1967) that economic demands of the emerging capitalist nations led to the slave trade and slavery. It seems that Morrison also favours his views. The fact that African-American people today are oppressed both because of their dark skin and their poverty clearly proves that race is a later justification for the enslavement of African-Americans. Morrison documents this by showing that Europeans and Native American Indians were enslaved before Africans. The European slave is represented by Miss Amy Denver of Boston. Denver says, "My mama worked for these here people to pay for her passage. But then she had me and since she died right after, well, they said I had to work for em to pay it off" (p. 33). There is a similarity between her experiences and Africans. She like Africans undergoes the same work experience and punishment. Like African-American slaves she too is denied education, making her English vernacular almost indistinguishable from that of the African slave.

In sum, their oppression is common. Morrison shows the Indian's willingness to make a home for run-away African slaves, allowing them to become a part of the tribe or to leave as they pleased:

> Buffalo-men, they [the Indians] called them, [the run away slaves]. . . . Nobody from a box in Alfred, Georgia, cared about the illness the Cherokee warned them about, so they stayed, all forty-six, resting, planning their next move. Paul D. had no idea of what to do and knew less than anybody it seemed. (p. 112)

So capitalism has been the primary enemy of all the three groups: the exploited European indentured servant, the native American Indian, and the African. Also the theft of raw materials for developing industrial countries and then the theft of a labour force to work within these countries have created the notions of inferiority and superiority leading to racism and sexism. According to Walter Rodney,

> The simple fact is that no people can enslave another for centuries without coming out with a notion of superiority, and when the colour and other physical traits of those peoples were quite different it was inevitable that the prejudice should take a racist form. (p. 100)

Morrison is successful in documenting slavery and its aftermath. She dexterously shows how slavery was always slavery on whether Sweet Home or any other plantation. The conditions of slavery were qualitatively indistinguishable whether the slave had a good master or bad master. For instance, Baby Suggs reveals how her slave life has been a continuous cycle of oppression. Her present like her past is intolerable. Even the life of free Africans in slave society, is not different either. Hence Morrison lays stress on collective struggle:

> Days of Company: knowing the names of forty, fifty other Negroes, their views, habits; where they had been and what done; of feeling their fun and sorrow along with her own, . . . at 124 and in the Clearing, along with others she [Sethe] had claimed herself. (p. 95)

It is absolutely right that the dark skin of slaves and their destitution are the causes of their hapless condition. For example, in order to purchase Baby Suggs' freedom Halle has to work for five years, even on Sundays. Baby Suggs is merely a breeding animal in the eyes of her master, which is why she does not object to Sethe's killing of her daughter. Solidarity is the only way in which African-American people can sustain themselves.

In this novel Morrison reinforces her theme of one people, one struggle and one solution. As Mbalia asserts,

> In *Beloved* life is hell, but togetherness, shared experience, and brotherly/sisterly love help the characters to survive, if not to forge better lives for themselves. (*Developing Class Consciousness,* p. 33)

According to Morrison African-American people living all over the world are one people, having the same history and problems, and they need to be united. *Beloved* makes it manifest that the condition of African-Americans in the United States stems from their class oppression, that their chief enemy is capitalism in all its disguises and the remedy to this problem lies in solidarity, not in a personal isolated struggle against capitalism. Morrison has been successful in her mission to make her fifth novel "unquestionably political and irrevocably beautiful".

In *Beloved,* Morrison uses mysticism and magic to

accentuate their intricacies as well as their manifold presence in African-American culture. Their multifaceted qualities are ever present throughout the text and visible in everything from her use of folk medicine—salt and spiderweb—to supernatural and folk belief: "You know as well as I do [Ella tells Stamp Paid] people who die bad don't stay in the ground" (p. 188). Their presence confirms if not crystallizes the fact that mysticism and magic are not only seminal in her collected works but often the centerpieces.

Morrison's *Beloved* has been described as "a ghost story about history." Thomas R. Edward is right in saying that Beloved "is no more apparition. She is solidly physical"; she is not a "projection of a neurotic observer, or a superstitious mass of delusion" (p. 18). The character Beloved is not just the ghost of Sethe's dead child; she is a succubus, a female demon and a nightmare figure that sexually assaults male sleepers and drains them off semen. The succubus figure, which is related to the vampire, another sexualized figure that drains a vital fluid, was incorporated into African-American folklore in the form of shape-shifting witches who "ride" their terrified victims in the night, and Beloved embodies the qualities of that figure as well. In separate assaults, Beloved drains Paul D. of semen and Sethe of vitality; symptomatically, Beloved's body swells as she also feeds off her victims' horrible memories of and recurring nightmares about sexual violations that occurred in their enslaved past. But Beloved functions as more than the receptacle of remembered stories; she reenacts sexual violation and thus figures the persistent nightmares common to survivors of trauma. Her insistent manifestation constitutes a challenge for the characters who have survived rapes inflicted while they were enslaved: directly, and finally communally, to confront a past they cannot forget. Indeed, it is apparent forgetting that subjects them to traumatic return; confrontation requires a direct attempt at remembering.

Morrison uses the succubus figure to represent the effects of institutionalized rape under slavery. When the enslaved persons' bodies were violated, their reproductive potential was commodified. The succubus, who rapes and steals semen, is metaphorically linked to such rapes and to the exploitation of African-Americans' reproduction. Just as rape was used to dehumanize enslaved persons, the succubus or vampire's assault robs victims of vitality, both physical and psychological. By representing a female rapist figure and a male rape victim, Morrison foregrounds race, rather than gender, as the category determining domination or subjugation to rape.

Beloved represents African-American history or collective memory as much as she does Sethe's or Paul's individual memory. The narrative merges Beloved's memories of death with the histories of women who endured the Middle Passage, where the institutionalized rape of enslaved women began. Both Sethe's mother and her mother's friend Nan are violated en route to North American slavery. Beloved remembers and recounts their horror:

> dead men lay on top of her. . . . [S]he had nothing to eat. Ghosts without skin stuck their fingers in her and said beloved in the dark and bitch in the light. (p. 241)

Morrison has explained in an interview that Beloved speaks "the language of both experiences, death and the Middle Passage" in this section and that the language "is the same" for both. ("Realm", p. 6) But Beloved is also speaking a revised language of rape structured by the historical narratives of rape in slavery. In Beloved's language White and Black are nouns rather than modifiers. Largely about men and women, the available idiom of rape in American culture has obfuscated the centrality of race. For instance, there is no widely recognizable story of White men's rape of Black women, and narratives of homosexual rape are even less visible when the victim is Black. The only recognizable narrative of interracial rape is what Angela Davis has called "the myth of the black rapist". (p. 172)

A potentially troublesome part of the novel is how Beloved is exorcised from 124. Paul D.'s initial driving of her spirit from the premises is merely temporary. She is finally exorcised not by individuals working in isolation but by a community of effort directed against her presence. And that community of effort comes from group of women, women who call upon ancient and contemporary messages, murmuring incantations and singing songs, to control Beloved. Is Morrison suggesting finally that women, who may themselves be demonic—or because they are demonic—are the only force with sufficient power to control that evil? Is it a question of good *versus* evil? Are the women who send Beloved away in any way identified with the forces of good? Most of them are certainly not the image of stereotypically traditional churchgoing Black women. Nor do they pursue the exorcism from altruistic motivations. Rather, like Richard Wright's District Attorney Ely Houston pursuing the murderous Cross Demon in *The Outsider* (1953), they are simultaneously attracted to and repulsed by the evil in their midst. They see in tiny mirrors of the selves they have suppressed, and they want extracted before it touches them too greatly or even has the potential to reclaim them. And they are offended. They "didn't mind a little communication between the two worlds, but this was an invasion". (p. 257)

In other words, Beloved is a threat to them in the psychological sphere as effectively as Sula is a threat to the women in the Bottom in the sexual sphere. Extending the philosophy from that nowhere the community is content to recognize evil and let it run course, the women in *Beloved* cannot afford that detachment. Let Beloved run her course may mean the destruction of them all. They must exorcise that part of themselves, therefore, that is a threat to them. If thy right eye offend thee, pluck it out. This is not a far-fetched philosophy when we consider that throughout history it is frequently women who cast sanctions most vehemently upon other women.

Exorcising the demonic part of the self so that all women are not judged to be demons—that is what the women are about on getting Beloved to leave 124. And how do they accomplish this? With a combination of pagan and religious rituals. They initially find power in numbers as they gather in a group of thirty to move toward 124. They raise their voices on singing and in religious murmurs as they march along the road. The comparative images that come to mind are straight out of *The Golden Bough*. The voices raised serve the same function as the sticks and pans villagers of pre-technological cultures might have used to drive evil spirits from their midsts. The act of singing itself serves as a chant, perhaps as the proverbial "witch doctor" of ancient times might have used to implore or command that some living/hearing evil take its leave from the environs of the innocent and the helpless.

Beloved's reincarnation is not surprising, as Morrison has always presented mystic and supernatural elements in her novels. For instance, in *The Bluest Eye* we have Soaphead Church, a spiritualist who uses magic in order to fulfil Pecola's desire of acquiring blue eyes. In *Sula* we have Eva's dreambook of numbers, her superstitions about attending a wedding in red attire, about the flock of black birds that marked Sula's coming back to the Bottom, and Ajax's conjuring mother. The navelless shaman Pilate in *Song of Solomon* keeps her deceased father's bones in her home and communicates with him. And in *Tar Baby* we have the visitation experience of Valerian Street.

Morrison's use of conventional myths and folk material is most visible in using the name of Sethe, which Morrison derives from Seth, who was one of the greater gods of ancient Egypt, and the biblical Seth, who was the Scion of Adam and Eve and whose descendants include Noah and his grandson Ham, who was denounced for having seen his grandfather naked. This biblical mythology is frequently used to justify the repression of African-Americans. It is the irony that we face when we consider the physical appearance of the Egyptian mythical Seth that is important to Morrison's use of the name. In form he was part man and part animal or bird; he was often connected with purification rituals.

Interestingly enough, what remains problematic for Morrison's Sethe is schoolteacher's concentration on her more "animalistic" characteristics in his effort to denigrate her and the other Sweet Home slaves. Yet, in reporting her action at the time she attempts to protect her children, Morrison's narrator describes Sethe's behaviour with birdlike images: Sethe "heard wings. Little hummingbirds stuck their needle beaks right through her headcloth into her hair and beat their wings. . . . She just flew". (p. 163) Also, when she thinks the grown Beloved is in danger,

> She hears wings. Little hummingbirds stick their needle beaks right through her headcloth into her hair and beat their wings. . . . She flies. (p. 262)

Sethe's indirect association with cows draws fully on the ancient mythologies and religion that her name suggests. We are told that while waiting for Sethe's arrival, the Sweet Home men wasted themselves on cows. After witnessing Halle's and Sethe's first sexual experience, Paul D. thinks, "The jump . . . from a calf to a girl wasn't all that mighty". (p. 26) Paul D would direct his most wounding remark at Sethe with images that presumably associate her with a cow: "You got two feet, Sethe, not four" (165).

Viewed strictly in the physionomystic realm of schoolteacher and the chattel world of economic slavery, the association of Sethe with an animal is at best insulting and at worst degrading, but viewed in the mythical and mystical world of ancient Egypt, one may come to envision a goddess such as Hathor, mother of the sun god, who had a human face but the ears and horns of a cow. In mythology, moreover, a cow is generally seen as the giver of life. Because of its fecundity, the cow, like the earth, is often mother goddess, nurturer and provider of food (milk), a life-giving source. Thus, by topsy-turvying the traditional negative stereotypes of chattel slavery, Morrison successfully elevates Sethe to the level of goddess through her selection of name alone.

Morrison's propensity to explore myths, mysticism, and magic—can be clearly seen from the above assessment. Her propensity to create, revise and rewrite her own provides clear insight into he use of Beloved as character. Sethe's slain daughter does indeed allow to probe any superficial boundaries between myth and reality, as Morrison might perceive them. More important, however, through her use of Beloved we find Morrison reaching deep into African-American oral folk culture not only to utilize one of the gems that lie at the very foundation of the more formal (written) African-American literary tradition but to demonstrate her talents as a master story teller.

In the end, Morrison's success in this novel must be viewed in relation to her use of the oral tradition of folk art in general, which would necessarily include the mystical. Her spontaneity and newness are key elements, for they contribute to the ultimate of the storyteller: to create a tale in which the process of telling the story is just as important as the tale itself.

6

Jazz: Towards an Understanding of the Black Self

After proposing the collective class struggle against the exploitative economic system in *Beloved*, Morrison emphasizes in *Jazz* the necessity of gender solidarity for African-American women in order to free themselves from gender atrocities. This novel adds a new dimension to the solution for oppressed African-American women. It is through female bonding and gender solidarity that African-American women can get over their problems and can help build a healthy and wholesome life. African-American women have always been separated from her men who were either sold during slavery or who left them when they went to seek jobs in the North. During Reconstruction, the African-American woman had to lean on other women in the community who became a "source of survival, information and psychic and emotional support" (Bethel, p. 179). African-American women's identification and solidarity, as Lorraine Bethel puts it,

> is most simply the idea of Black women seeking their own identity and defining themselves through bonding on various levels – psychic, intellectual and emotional as well as physical – with other Black women. (Murthy, p. 82)

The theme of women bonding is not new in Morrison's novels, but Mbalia has correctly pointed out "it is a jazz melody plucked anew and given prominence by the musician who is Morrison". ("Women who Run with Wild", p. 635)

Morrison exploits the mode of jazz to reveal the experience of African-American society during the 1920s, the Jazz Age. She uses her fiction as a framework for investigating the manifold oppression of African-Americans and finding remedies to their situation. Through this novel she wants to convey the message that gender solidarity is the ultimate remedy of gender oppression.

As the plot of *Beloved* had been derived from a newspaper clipping, similarly Morrison took the seed of this story from Camille Billop's manuscript, *The Harlem Book of Dead*, which contains pictures and commentary by the eminent African-American photographer, James Van Der Zee with poems by Owen Dodson. Van Der Zee describes the curious origins of his photograph of a young woman's corpse:

> She was the one I think was shot by her sweetheart at a party with a noiseless gun. She complained of being sick at the party and friends said, "Well, why don't you lay down?" And they taken her in the room and laid her down. After they undressed her and loosened her clothes, they saw the blood on her dress. They asked her about it and she said, "I'll tell you tomorrow, yes, I'll tell you tomorrow". Yes, I'll tell you tomorrow". She has just trying to give him a chance to get away. (Gates and Appiah, 53)

As she lay dying, the young girl refused to identify her assassin. Morrison planned to write a novel based on this story, and after ten years it became possible. It seems that *Jazz* is meant to follow *Beloved* as the second volume of a trilogy. Still it is not just an extension of the story narrated in *Beloved* in a conventional way, for the characters and the location are new. The narrative approach is also different. Morrison wishes to tell in her trilogy-in-progress the tale of

African-American people passing through their American experience from the days of slavery to the present.

In her novels, Morrison emphasizes the necessity for African-Americans to see themselves within a culture. The very title of this novel, *Jazz,* restates the nature of her inspiration. In *Jazz,* an African-American man murders an African-American girl for her betrayal in love. Here her treatment of theme seems slightly different. The characters are all urban and city dwellers. Her narrative approach is unique. It has always been her mission to make her people conscious of their cultural heritage. The novel tells the sad story of Violet and Joe Trace. It is the first time Morrison keeps a couple, Joe Trace and Violet, at centre stage who were married for over two decades. As in her other novels the narrative navigates between present and past to the rural Virginia of the 1880s where Joe and Violet met and from which they ultimately moved to the magical place they love to call the city. As the story unfolds we begin to understand what happened.

Like several jazz pieces, the novel has a fast beginning, establishing a dominant note and theme and then breaks into various parts: various stories (passages) and voices (instruments), various motifs, images and relative themes. Just as in the novel, jazz pieces return again and again to the dominant subject of human passion.

Through a precise use of the jazz idiom, Morrison narrates the tale of Joe Trace, a 50-year-old salesman of Cleopatra cosmetics, and his spouse, Violet, a hairdresser, both of whom had moved to New York City in 1926, leaving behind all the sad memories of their childhood: "When all the wars are over and there will never be another". (p. 7) In the middle of the post-war euphoria, the African-American community receives a jolt when Joe Trace kills his paramour, Dorcas, because she leaves him at a party for a boy Acton. His wife then crashes Dorcas's funeral and disfigures her face with a knife. To find out why any of this has happened, all of it summarized on the first page of *Jazz,* we will have to listen to the end of Morrison's song, "as if Sidney Bechet had met the Archduke Trio; as if Ellington had gone Baroque" (Leonard, p. 14).

African-Americans are bound by both history and culture. In *The Bluest Eye,* Claudia realizes that Maureen Peal is not her enemy inasmuch as both of them belong to the same community in that they are taught that beauty has to be measured by the standards of the ruling class:

> And all the time we knew that Maureen Peal was not the enemy and not worthy of such intense hatred. The thing to fear was the Thing that made her beautiful, and not us". (p. 58)

In *Sula,* Nel comes to realize the truth of Eva's words: "You Sula what's the difference?" (p. 168) Although both are from drastically dissimilar social backgrounds, they are bound by factors much more powerful than those which tend to divide them. Milkman in *Song of Solomon* sees himself as a part of a community in Michigan and in Shalimar as a prerequisite to becoming a part of his living. In *Tar Baby* Jadine's isolation from her folks, including her aunt Ondine and uncle Sydney, makes her more a tanned European ("Copper Venus") than an African-American girl. In *Beloved* Sethe relies on the African-American community in order to purge the phantom from 124: "Unloaded, 124 is just another weathered house needing repair". (p. 164) The alliance between African-Americans is not new in Morrison's fiction.

Morrison in *Jazz* transposes music into another medium, the novel, in which the music that was created by her people revealed their happiness and sorrows, their convictions and their psyche. Just as this music—spirituals, blues, ragtime, and jazz—has spread throughout the world in our time and is no longer uniquely or exclusively African-American, Morrison realizes that there is a need now to make a novel do what the music used to do and tell the whole world the ongoing story of her people. Hence her fictions do not only narrate but also sing those origin myths and archetypes of African-Americans in the U.S.A. which is what Zora Neale Hurston has done in her novel, *Their Eyes were Watching God.*

Other great writers such as Paule Marshall, Gwendolyn Brooks, James Baldwin, Richard Wright and Ralph Ellison have also done similar things.

For that matter, we can say that Morrison is a jazz musician, "not only because she signifies, assimilates, and advances the themes and structures of great African works, but also and primarily because she signifies, assimilates and advances the themes and structures of her own canon". ("Women who Run with Wild", p. 623) *Jazz* continues this custom of signifying, assimilating and advancing the mutuality of theme and structure. As in jazz, the story and the narrating of the story are one; similarly in *Jazz*, theme and structure merge to suggest the unity that must prevail among African-American women. First we are made conscious of the unifying process in the novel's inscription:

> I am the name of the sound
> and the sound of the name.
> I am the sign of the letter
> and the designation of the division.
>
> (Epithet to the Novel, *Jazz*)

From this it is clear that nothing is inseparable and distinct and that theme is structure, and structure is theme. Morrison provides us with yet another clue to the unifying process in the first word of the novel—"Sth". This word or sound like "buzz" is both the name of the sound and the sound of the name as suggested in the inscription of the novel. Thus, the message of gender solidarity through female bonding cannot be conveyed in a better way than in jazz, a music form in which songster, song, and song telling are one and the same. Like great jazz musicians, Morrison's genius in *Jazz* lies in removing the divisions between theme and structure. As in jazz the narrator is not detached from the story he is narrating, so in *Jazz* the narrator is not separate from the story she is narrating.

It is the story of African-American women that Morrison is most anxious to present, because it is only they who experience the triple threat of race, gender and class. She raises a current issue confronting African-Americans, relates it to problems African-Americans faced during 1920s and shows that the solution then and now remains the same.

All African-American people were in danger of exploitive conditions caused by the changing U.S. economy in the 1920s, an economy that moved rapidly from a slavocracy to industrialism but maintained the racism that this economy spawned. The results were the worst race riots in the history of America. If conditions for all African-American people were barbaric and wild, then conditions for African-American women were downright war-like, for, unlike African-American men, African-American women were also in danger from the sexism that, like racism, is spawned and supported by capitalism.

Conditions of African-American women were no better in the South than in the North. The main reason parents gave for sending their daughters north was fear of molestation. As Jacqueline Jones asserts:

> Significantly black men mentioned the degraded status of their women folk as one of the prime incentives to migrate, along with low wages and poor educational opportunities for their children. Husband told of sexual harassment of wives and daughters by White men and of other forms of indignities woven into the fabric of Southern society. (p. 157)

Whether in the cities of the North like New York or in the cities of the South, all were the same for women:

> Every week since Dorcas' death, during the whole of January and February, a paper laid bare the bones of some broken women. Man kills wife. Eight accused of rape dismissed. Women and girl victims of. Woman commits suicide. White attackers indicted. . . . In jealous rage man. (p. 74)

So while migrating to the North, African-American women thought that they would be free from all sorts of exploitation, but they were actually unaware of the fact that race and gender discrimination were alive as much in there as in the South. Hence the dire need for gender solidarity among African-American women.

Along with racism and sexism, Morrison emphasizes female bonding in this novel more than other previous novels. Of course, she has talked about this subject in her all novels. For instance in *The Bluest Eye* Claudia yearns of the "Security and warmth of Big Mama's Kitchen". (p. 15) In *Sula*, Nel has been to Sula the closest thing. In *Song of Solomon*, Pilate becomes a source of strength for Ruth to fend off Macon Dead. In *Tar Baby*, Jadine's identification with African-American women at Eloe as the "Other" leads to a discovery of the self. In *Beloved*, Sethe finds Baby Suggs as a cultural mentor who kindles a passion in her to know her past and to love herself as a human being. In *Jazz*, Violet too learns valuable lessons in the company of Dorcas, Alice Manfred and Felice. They bring a drastic change to her. Unlike Jadine in *Tar Baby*, who relinquishes her culture and solidarity with African-American women, Violet accepts the influence of various African-American women in her life. Dorcas, Alice and Felice not only lead her to self-discovery but also help her work on her relationship with Joe.

Violet's violent act of disfiguring Dorcas's face at the funeral stuns the entire community, but it is the women who empathize with her. Malvonne, her neighbour, confesses to Joe that although she dislikes Violet's "violent" act, she cannot turn her back on another African-American woman. She tells him, "Okay, there's no love lost between Violet and me, but I take her part not yours" (p. 46). Violet has never met Dorcas. Her "memory is a sickness in the house—everywhere and nowhere" (28). Having to live with her memory, Violet realizes that she is falling in love with Dorcas:

> When she isn't trying to humiliate Joe, she is admiring the dead girl's hair; when she isn't cursing Joe.... she is having whispered conversations with the corpse in her head. (p. 15)

Violet reminds us of Sethe in *Beloved*. Sethe, after taking the life of her daughter Beloved, feels guilty of murder; similarly the photograph of Dorcas serves the same purpose in *Jazz*. It becomes a symbol of Violet's guilt. For rectifying her mistake, she decides to learn about Dorcas. As she learns the details of Dorcas's life, she feels that she could have been the daughter she never had. Violet begins to love and appreciate her. As Yamini K. Murthy suggests,

> Violet's relationship with Dorcas becomes an affirmation of love of one woman for another, although Violet starts out with hatred in her heart. (p. 82)

Violet's identification with African-American women like Dorcas slowly leads her to seek the real "me". She learns many precious lessons in the company of Dorcas's aunt, Alice Manfred, who earlier declined to meet her. Violet's repeated and insistent efforts to meet her finally pay off. Alice previously assumes that she wants to seek forgiveness, but when Violet finally meets her, she is willing to sit with and talk to her. She says that she "had to sit down somewhere. I thought I could do it here" (p. 82). Very soon an intimacy develops between them, and Violet becomes the only visitor she ever "looked forward to". Though in the beginning they are apprehensive of each other, gradually both start to understand one another. Now Alice starts to talk to Violet in a way she has never done with anyone. She forgives her and soon "the women. . . became so easy with each other, talk wasn't always necessary". (p. 112) More importantly, Alice and Violet learn to laugh and learn that "laughter is serious. . . more complicated, more serious than tears". (p. 113). At last, Violet convinces Alice as to why she had to mutilate the dead body of Dorcas. She makes Alice realize that she, a woman who has never held a knife to harm others, would certainly fight and murder for her man. After this Alice is able to understand Violet's violent act in disfiguring Dorcas's corpse. So the friendship of Alice helps Violet define herself and become more self-confident.

Violet learns the meaning of life from Alice. Now she

understands that she has been denying herself all along and that she has to make the most of it. Alice teaches her how to love: "You got anything left to you to love, any thing at all, do it". (p. 112) It is not surprising that Violet identifies herself completely with Alice, and with this identification, she establishes her own individuality and becomes a person even Joe learns to love and admire.

As Violet needs the company of Alice, Alice too needs the company of Violet. From her, Alice learns that despite belonging to different classes African-American women are similar, and they face the same problems of race, gender and class. The only two classes that exist are the owner capitalist class and the subject worker class. This becomes clear from the conversation between Violet and Alice:

"They're just women, you know. Like us. . . ."

"Don't they fight all the time, when you do their hair?"

"You're not afraid they might start fighting?"

"Only when they sober", Violet smiled.

"Oh, well."

"They share men, fight them and fight over them, too."

"No woman should live like that."

"No. No woman should have to". (p. 84)

From this conversation it is clear that both poor, uneducated African-American women and educated middle-class African-American women are oppressed due to the

Alice learns not only from Violet's teaching but also from her own voice. She speaks her mind to Violet, develops a wild tongue and "lets the wild come up and out". Through this cathartic process, she learns about herself. This bonding helps them not only to converse but also to cry and to laugh; all three are signs of healing. Alice teaches Violet how to laugh at herself:

Crumpled over, shoulders shaking, Violet thought

> about how she must have looked at the funeral, at what her mission was. The sight of herself trying to do something bluesy, something hep, fumbling the knife, too late any way. . . . She laughed till she coughed and Alice had to make them a cup of settling tea. (p. 114)

After this act of observing herself objectively, Violet becomes whole again.

Along with Alice, Violet helps Felice, Dorcas's girl friend, to review her life. Felice arrives at the Trace household to fetch her lost ring but stays not only to discover her own self but also to understand her relationship with her mother. With Violet, Felice feels at home. This is the first time in her life when she does not hesitate to reveal her past. As Denver and other African-American women in the community help Beloved in *Beloved* to realize that her mother's act of infanticide was necessitated by her love, because her mother does not want to see her daughter in the shackles of slavery, Violet tries to make Felice realize that her mother stole a ring from the shop only out of "out of spite". (p. 203) Violet's intimacy with Felice helps her understand her mother Rose and her grandmother True Belle better. Above all, Felice's coming into Violet's home re-establishes harmony there. Violet's understanding of the self leads her to establish a harmonious relationship with her husband by sharing personal things again in their married life. Thus "as Violet, Alice and Felice come together as African-American women, and discover their own selves through bonding with other African-American women, they come to an end of a pilgrimage to know and be their own true selves". (Murthy, p. 81) When each one comes to this realization, they learn not only the techniques of how to live but also how to dream. Mainly, Violet reaches the end of her pilgrimage in discovering herself.

Through this unity, African-American women became more than close friends. In nurturing each other, each becomes a "mama" for the other. As Mbalia points out, "what Violet, Alice, Dorcas, and Felice have in common is the need for 'mamas'". ("Women who Run with Wild", p. 634) Violet's mother commits suicide, Dorcas' mother is assassinated, and Felice's mother is absent. That is why they all utter the word "mama" during a crisis: "'Oh, Mama'. Alice Manfred blurted it out and then covered her mouth. Violet had the same thought. Mama. Mama?" (p. 110). When Dorcas was dying and people asked her her killer's name, she replies, "I know his name but Mama won't tell" (p. 193). Luckily, Felice finds in Violet a "mama" just in time: "I can see why Mrs. Manfred let [Violet] visit. She doesn't lie, Mrs. Trace. Nothing she says is a lie the way it is with most older people" (p. 105).

Morrison, in *Jazz,* shows how African-American women benefit from each other's companionship. She successfully minimizes gender atrocities through female bonding. As a skilled novelist, she drives home to us the need for sisterhood in the African-American community through which communication, not silence, will forge the way toward a healthy, wholesome future.for all people of African descent, particularly women.

7

Paradise: Paradise Found and Lost

Toni Morrison's mission is to project and highlight the victimization of African-Americans, especially women. Like *Jazz* she emphasizes the importance of gender solidarity in *Paradise*, her first novel after winning the Nobel Prize for literature in 1993. It is the third in the series of her novels exploring themes from African-American history. *Beloved* is about slavery, *Jazz* deals with urban life in the jazz era, and *Paradise* is set in contemporary times. It is inspired by stories of the all-African-American communities that were established after slavery came to an end. About the idea of the story Morrison writes,

> Part of my idea came precisely from that research and thinking about that whole period when ex-slaves, freed-men, life plantations—sometimes under duress because southerners frequently wanted them to stay – but managed to take advantage of the land that was offered in places like Oklahoma, and to build whole towns, churches, stores, banks, many houses. And some of them are still there to see. (Kakutani, p. 1)

The book begins with the question: "How do fierce, revolutionary, moral people lose it and become destructive and static—exactly what they were running from?" Morrison states,

> I was thinking about certain people, African-Americans on the public scene, who had abandoned and changed their political beliefs after thirty or forty years. Everyone says that happens as one ages. That such passions are only the passions of youth. The associated question was whether the fight, when one is young, for social justice or for the good life is a struggle for a kind of paradise where everything is the way it ought to be. It made me start to think about the whole concept of Paradise, so that the book became an interrogation of the idea of *Paradise,* (Verdilla, p. 7)

Paradise also explores the external struggle between men and women. Morrison focuses on the tensions that bubbled up during the late 1960s and 1970s, when women's roles were changing.

Ruby and the Convent offer two opposing visions of *Paradise*. Ruby has the features of the *Old Testament.* It is patriarchal. The men are very concerned about their roles as leaders and very protective of their women. The Convent women are running away from all kinds of trauma. They don't seek the company of men because they have been hurt by them. Even though they quarrel among themselves, they consider the convent a free place, a place where they don't have to fear that they are people to be preyed upon. The values of Ruby and Convent, therefore, are different. In Ruby there is a very profound protestant religion, while in the Convent there is a non-institutional form of religion verging on magic. The women represent the liberated women of the 1970s, and the conservative African-American community is insulted and horrified by them.

Paradise is a religious novel. In *Beloved* we see parental love, the love of a mother for her child. In *Jazz* there is romantic love, the love between Joe and Dorcas. But in *Paradise* there is love of God for fellow human beings. Religion has been profoundly important to African-Americans. So in *Paradise* Morrison juxtaposes "Organized religion and unorganized magic as two systems" (Deirure, p. 3). The tensions between the two result in tragedy.

More important than the issue of victimization in this novel is the danger inherent in attempting to create a paradise on earth that demands exclusion. The main point of the novel is the construction of an isolated community that can't survive.

The characters in this novel are both victims and victimizers. They are placed under tremendous stress. African-American men must protect their women and children from hostile Whites and from an unforgiving world where an African-American person's death is rarely mourned. These circumstances force the men to be hard, strong and merciless toward outsiders of every colour. As for the Convent women, they are mostly an assortment of fugitives: Connie, a former ward of the nuns who ran the Convent when it was a boarding school for Indian girls; Mavis, a paranoid woman who deserts her domineering husband in the Cart; Gigi, a seductive young woman whose boyfriend is in jail; Seneca, who has survived abandonment and sexual exploitation; and Pallas, a wealthy lawyer's daughter whose lover left her for her mother. Nearly every one of these characters is two-dimensional. Unlike the heroine of *Beloved*, who was strong, desperate, loving, vulnerable and angry all at once, almost all the women in this novel are victims. They have spent years grappling with economic hardships, romantic disappointment, social disparity and the stupid cruelties of men. The men, on the other hand, are almost uniformly control freaks, eager to dismiss independent women as witches and determined to make everyone submit to their will. Hence almost all the women are somehow racially and sexually oppressed.

Mavis is trapped inside her family. When she goes to purchase some meat for her husband, she unfortunately locks the car with all the windows closed, and her twin babies, Merle and Pearl, suffocate to death in it. Her family does not understand her situation or her grief and turn against her. They blame her for the death of the twins and start to torture her both mentally and physically. Her daughter, Sal digs into her side with her sharp nails until she can feel the blood and the pain. She doesn't dare swat Sal's hand away or acknowledge the pain even slightly. Instead, she "scratched the corner of her mouth". (p. 23)

Mavis doesn't even dare to react when Sal stomps her foot on the pretext of killing a beetle. The comfort and security of family life is denied to her as she learns to dread her own husband and children:

> Sal had Frank's old shaving razor unfolded by her plate and asked her father a series of questions, all starting with "Is it sharp enough to cut. . . ?" And Frank would answer, "cut anything from chin hair to gristle", or "cut the eyelashes off a bedbug", eliciting peals of laughter from Sal. When Billy James spit Kool-Aid into Mavis' plate . . . she didn't think it would take them long, and seeing how they were at supper, enjoying each other's jokes and all, she knew Frank would let the children do it. (p. 25)

Thus, the terrorized Mavis is sure that her own family will punish her for the death of the babies. Even her own mother does not trust her. According to her Mavis has become mad. So she rings up Frank and asks him to come and take Mavis "pronto". Finding herself unable to prove her sanity, Mavis flees. After leaving her home she reaches the Convent where she finds peace and "a swept world. Unjudgemental. Tidy. Ample. Forever". (p. 48)

The reader meets with the other three women who have internalized their oppression. Pain, violence and deprivation form the essential content of these women's lives. They are suspended in time and place; their life choices are so severely limited that the women themselves feel destroyed. They have attempted to escape from a world predicated upon the denigrated images of African-American womanhood. Seneca, deserted by her unwed mother, moves from one foster home to another. She has learnt to be silent, to keep her feelings to herself. She feels that she can never express her natural feelings of sorrow and hurt, because people always blame her for all that she suffers; she "knew it was something inside (her) that was the matter" (p. 261). Once, in one of her foster homes, a boy called Harry molested her. In the process of yanking on her jeans, a safety pin scratched her stomach. The foster mother, Mama Greer, was concerned about the cut and blood but ordered her not to say a word about Harry's behaviour to anyone. She was badly reprimanded: "Don't you ever say that again. Do you hear me? Do you? Nothing like that happens here." After having her favourite food, "She was placed in another home" (p. 261). Thus, shame and sorrow are internalized and she develops the masochistic tendency of surgically slicing her own body under her clothes until blood flows freely. The reader cannot blame Seneca, because she feels that this is the only alternative that she has in her attempt to escape her painful life.

Grace or Gigi, as she is called, is flamboyant and brazen. Unwanted by both parents, she is left alone in the world. She searches for stability and love that have been denied her in family life. Her quest is transmuted into carnal desire and involvement with men, which has resulted in disillusionment. She wears a "couldn't care less" attitude, which actually serves to camouflage her insecurity and pain and the incurable romantic in her.

Pallas Truelove elopes from her school with the Janitor, Carlos. She leaves the home of her rich and dominant father for the home of her painter mother with Carlos. Divine, Pallas's mother, is about the same age as Carlos, and they become attracted to each other. Pallas, who had felt secure in Carlos's love and had given herself to him in complete abandon, feels betrayed by both her lover and mother. The selfishness of a mother, who had once deserted her, dawns on her for a second time. She runs away from the traumatic situation, is chased and raped by some hoodlums, and then crashes into a lake. Later, she is rescued by some Indians who help her reach the hospital. She is in such a state of shock that she is unable to stop shivering and constantly relives her experience in the dirty cold water. The moment she wants to break her silence and speak, she falls again into the coldness of the lake, the trauma associated with it and the icy pits of language itself:

> So there. She had opened her lips a tiny bit to say two words, and no black water had seeped in. The cold still shook her bones, but the dark water had receded. For now. At night, of course, it would return and she would be back in it - trying not to think about what Swam below her neck. It was the top of the water she concentrated on and the flashlight licking the edge, then darting farther out over the black glimmer. Hoping, hoping the things touching below were sweet little goldfish like the ones in the bowl her father brought her when she was five. Or guppies, angles. Not alligators or snakes. This was a lake not a swamp or the aquarium at the San Diego Zoo. Floating over the water, the whispers were closer than their calls. "Here, pussy. Here, pussy. Kitty, kitty, kitty", sounded far away; but "Gimme the flash, dick-face, izzat her, let go, may be she drowned, no way," slid into the skin behind her ears. (p. 163)

Pallas had lived a secure life in the house of her father and now her quest for love and independence have left her traumatized and terrorized. Billie Delia discovers her at the hospital, takes pity on her and brings her to the safety and security of the Convent. It is a place where she can stay for a while. It is a place where the women are nice and never ask any questions. The women there are absolutely relaxed and never pry into anyone's business: "you can collect yourself there, think things through, withnothing or nobody bothering you all the time. They'll take care of you or leave you alone - whichever way you want it". (p. 176)

In the company of Mavis, Seneca and Gigi, Pallas finds comfort. Connie is the matriarch, authoritative yet never hegemonic nor domineering. She soothes each one and offers them the affection they crave, at the same time encouraging them towards acquiring a positive self-image. The domination suffered by the women in the Convent has been uniformly negative. Their knowledge of self emerges from their struggle to reject images and incidents that have threatened to maim them psychologically and physically. They parlay their anger into armour of survival. They have consciously distanced themselves from familiar situations. The Convent is the location where the women find the ideal space wherein they can be free and feel a blessed malelessness. It is essential for them to integrate personal knowledge, i.e., a kind of internal knowledge essential to African-American women's survival. Interspersing the roles of mother, daughter, sister and friend to one another, these African-American women affirm one another's humanity.

Mavis, Grace, Seneca and Pallas, all victims of various social discriminations, adhere to a cult of secrecy under the tutelage of Connie. They resort to "loud dreaming" in the darkness of the Cellar. The "loud dreaming" helps protect the sanctity of the inner aspects of their individual lives. It offers them a psychic space and allows them a positive self-image. At the beginning they draw designs around their naked bodies as they lie on the cold floor of the Cellar. Then encouraged by Connie they speak coherently and incoherently of things dead and long gone. These are "undone by murmurs of love" from others:

> That is how the loud dreaming began. How the stories rose in that place. Half-tales and the never-dreamed escaped from their lips to soar high above guttering Candles, shifting dust from crates and bottles. And it was never important to know who said the dream or whether it had meaning. In spite of or because their bodies ache, they step easily into the dreamer's tale. They enter the heat in the Cadillac, feel the smack of cold air in the Higgledy Piggledy. They know their tennis shoes are unlaced and that a bra strap annoys each time it slips from the shoulder. The Armour package is sticky. They inhale the perfume of sleeping infants and feel parent-cozy

> although they notice one's head is turned awkwardly. They adjust the sleeping baby head then refuse, outright refuse, what they know and drive away home. They climb porch stairs carrying frankfurters and babies and purse in their arms. Saying, "They don't seem to want to wake up, Sal, Sal? Look here. They don't seem to want to." They kick their legs under water, but not too hard for fear of waking fins or scales also down below. The male voices saying, saying forever, saying push their own down their throats. Saying, saying until hue is no breath to scream or contradict. Each one blinks and gags from tear gas, moves her hand slowly to the scraped shin, the torn ligament. Runs up and down the halls by day, sleeps in a ball with the lights on at night. Folds the five hundred dollars in the foot of her sock. Yelps with pain from a stranger's penis and a mother's rivalry - alluring and corrosive as Cocaine. (p. 264)

This is their way of exorcising the hurt. It is therapeutic. Thus their inner calm becomes externally visible. Now Seneca does not cut her body anymore; instead, she draws cross-marks in red on the template suggesting her body. Consolata does not need to cover her eyes with dark glasses. They have suddenly become adult and calm. They are "sociable and connecting" when they have visitors; "otherwise they were still and appraising". (p. 266) They cling to their secrets, which is the only way they can parlay their anger and hurt into a positive calm.

Morrison is continuously having her characters spell out the meaning of her story: "They think they have outfoxed the White-man when in fact they imitate him". (p. 306) She writes towards the end of the novel,

> They think they are protecting their wives and children, when in fact they are maiming them. And when the maimed children ask for help, they look elsewhere for the cause. Born out of an old hatred, one that began when one kind of black man scorned

> another kind and that kind took the hatred to another level, their selfishness had trashed two hundred years of suffering and triumph in a moment of such pomposity and error and callousness it froze the mind. (p. 306)

Ruby, she adds, was,

> A backward, noplace ruled by men whose power to control was out of control and who had the nerve to say who could live and who not and where; who had seen in lively, free, unarmed females the mutiny of the mares and so got rid of them. (p. 308)

Having internalized, at least in part, the entrenched Puritan heritage of White America, Ruby views the Convent sceptically at best, even though its official ties to Catholicism have long been severed. In addition, because Ruby's male leaders are unable to see the parallels that exist between the patriarchal structures of their town and of Catholicism, they view with suspicion the idea of convents and nuns and, in particular, the idea of women who have chosen deliberately to abstain from sexual relations with men and thus to forego reproduction; they cannot make the connection between their own and Catholicism's maintenance of power precisely through the regulation of women's sexuality and reproductive capacity. In effect, the town of Ruby actively sets up the Convent as a dangerous separatist space in order to keep the Convent women outside its own boundaries. However, the real dogmatic, separatist enclave is Ruby itself, whose leaders work hard to construct the Convent in binary opposition to itself.

Paradise carefully delineates the history of this town as one created by former slave men who had been discriminated against not only by Whites but also by "Negro towns" (13) and who in response chose a separatism that became discrimination against all others. The freedmen became a tight band of wayfarers bound by the enormity of what had happened to them. Their horror of Whites was convulsive but abstract. They saved the clarity of their hatred for the African-American men who had insulted them in ways too confounding for language: first by excluding them, then by offering them staples to exist in that very exclusion.

That this exclusion by other "Negroes" is grounded in skin colour, in "light-skinned against black", is a revelation to the "8-rock males". They immediately understand the "serious consequences" of this racial "difference" in terms of patriarchal power: "Serious enough that their daughters would be shunned as brides; their sons chosen last" (p. 194). Their response to this insulting rebuff by "fair-skinned coloured men. Blue-eyed, grey-eyed yellowmen" (p. 195) is to be found their own "all-black" (p. 5) town, Haven (and later Ruby, after Haven withers), grounded in dogmatic racist and patriarchal terms that simply reverse the hierarchy of the racism they themselves suffered by excluding all who are not so dark as themselves.

In Haven and then Ruby, the "Fathers" rule and the darkest "8-rock" (p. 194), coal-black skin is privileged; others are driven away or marginalized. Holding onto the logic of hierarchical opposition, the town must continually enforce its borders, given that defining an identity, a closed totality, always depends on excluding some elements. As Pat Best recognizes, "people get chosen and ranked" based upon "skin color" in Ruby (p. 216). For example, the community forces Menus to "return the women he brought home to marry. The pretty sandy-haired girl from Virginia" (p. 195) and marginalizes Roger Best's wife (Delia), daughter (Pat), and granddaughter (Bellia Delia) for their "sunlight skin" (p. 196), which marks them as other. Marginalization functions as a form of violence when Delia dies because no one will get her the medical help she needs. The "fastest girl in town" (p. 59) label accentuates and casts a deprecatory shadow onto Bellia Delia's racial otherness, and she eventually leaves Ruby. That these examples are all women is not surprising, given that the town patriarchs consolidate their power through an unspoken but extremely tight control over reproduction and thus over women. As Pat recognizes, "Everything that worries them must come from women", in that "the generations had to be not only racially untampered with but free of adultery too" (p. 217) in order to ensure racial purity. Bellia Delia recognizes that the rumors and verbal battles between the men that ensue when Arnette is found pregnant out of wedlock and then loses the baby have to do with "disobedience, which meant, of course, the stallions were fighting about who controlled the mares and their foals". (p. 150)

The town patriarchs' suspicion and fear of the women living in the Convent on the outskirts of the town is also a function of their desire to retain control over their separatist enclave, grounded in racial purity and enforced through a patriarchal and racist ideology allowing for no dissenting views. Indeed, the novel traces the trajectory of this unforgiving and dogmatic separatism, and the patriarchal power attached to it, to its logical murderous conclusion, given that "neither the founders of Haven nor their descendants could tolerate anybody but themselves" (p. 13). As Pat puts it, the men resort to violence to rid the Convent of its women residents not only because they see the women as impure and unholy but mainly "because they could— which is what being an 8-rock meant to them" (p. 297). Power and violence are interlaced for the town's patriarchs, given that their source of power depends on absolute power over women and their reproductive capacities.

Although clearly offering a critique of the town's racist, patriarchal, separatist structure and ideology as incompatible with any kind of coalition work that seeks to re-imagine justice not only as fair but also as nurturing and non-hierarchical, *Paradise* nevertheless indicates the necessity at times of separatism for survival and the limited possibilities of coalition within a separatist structure. Indeed, when first founded, the town of Haven does operate in the spirit of coalition, in basic sense that its citizens help each other survive: Its "residents refused each other nothing, were vigilant to any need or shortage" (p. 109). Having been rebuffed from all sides, they regroup and found their own thriving town. However, this caring coalition is so rigidly circumscribed, operating only with respect to the chosen families and excluding outsiders on the basis of skin colour, that it cannot survive. A place in which "outsider" and "enemy" "mean the same thing" (p. 212) and in which the "Fathers" rule with absolute power cannot sustain the spirit of coalition. Predictably, Haven collapses, with too many offspring choosing to desert. However, the sons of the original founders and fathers regroup and move elsewhere to start the experiment all over again, founding the town of Ruby and believing once again that they were "on their way to Paradise" (p. 202). The problem is that Ruby replicates Haven in all ways and is thus doomed to repeat its failures: It thrives while it is being constructed in the spirit of coalition but slowly evolves into a fascist enclave when keeping its own in and others out becomes its primary means of ensuring its identity and survival at all costs.

Although the novel presents the ideals of the Civil Rights Movement as a means of getting past the dead end that Haven and then Ruby represent, *Paradise* also engages in a critique of the patriarchal aspects of the movement and the limitations that result as a consequence of these aspects. The novel's presentation of Misner as working to bring battling factions in the town together to negotiate truces and to give voice to the young people of the town illustrates the possibilities of the Civil Rights movement's ideal of participatory democracy in moving away from a power dynamic that gives power to the few and functions through the threat of violence. For example, Misner attempts to teach the young people "strategies of defence. Not aggression. Defense". However, his work is made difficult by their inability to "know the difference" (p. 208), as Pat points out to him, given that their world-view has been constructed within an extreme hierarchical, patriarchal context that does not flinch from resorting to violence to ensure its dominance. Indeed, Misner himself remains caught within a tightly woven patriarchal structure that seriously limits the possibilities for change that he wishes to promote. As a male preacher,

Misner inherently holds power in a town and culture that privilege men and fathers as well as religious structure that is itself deeply patriarchal. Indeed, Misner's Baptist church boasts "the largest congregation in town as well as the most powerful" (p. 56-57), so that even the most powerful town patriarchs, Deacon and Stewart Morgan, are forced to reign in their suspicions of the men and at times bend to his will. Although Misner's authority as a Baptist minister allows him to bring together the various interested parties after the altercation between Amette and K.D. in an attempt to put into practice the ideals of participatory democracy and non-violence, the attempt remains seriously flawed in its exclusion of women. Ideally, participatory democracy involves extensive and active engagement of citizens in the self-governing process, in a direct fashion day in and day out, in all matters that affect them in their common lives, and thus involves collective deliberation and ongoing accommodation. However, Amette is glaringly absent from the meeting of "those concerned," as in her mother, whereas K.D. is present along with "his uncles Deek and Stewart, Reverend Misner, Amette's father and brother" (p. 54).

Misner's meeting thus reinforces the dogmatic patriarchal structure of the town, in which women are denied a voice and, indeed, remain possessions of men that must be negotiated by men. Although the men pay lip service to the influence of women, as when Amette's father Jeff claims that "my wife's the key" and Deacon Morgan agrees that "women always the key", the men essentially silence and exclude the women from negotiations and decisions. *Paradise* foregrounds this exclusion when Misner closes the meeting with a prayer and the men hear "the tippy-tap steps of women who were nowhere to be seen" (p. 61). Misner's actions are emblematic of the Civil Rights movement's patriarchal structure, in which officers of the leading organizations were male African-American ministers who didn't allow women into their ranks even though women were not only very active but also highly influential within the day-to-day running of these organizations as well as in setting the agenda of the movement and constructing a model of participatory democracy. Moreover, that Misner organises an all-male meeting indicates a sexist assumption of male superiority that women within the movement complained about and that was most fully exemplified by Stokley Carmichael's now infamous comment that "the only position for women in SNCC is prone" (Evans, pp. 234, 87). Even as he participates in excluding women from the coalition work he promotes, however, Misner has inklings of the exclusions of many from official versions of the Movement; he reflects that "all sorts of people will claim pivotal, controlling, defining positions in the rights movement", that "a few would be justified", but that "the ordinary folk", "would be forgotten" even though "they were the ones who formed the spine on which the televised ones stood" (p. 212). The character of Misner thus serves multiple functions as a means of presenting both the complexities and limitations of the Civil Rights Movement.

However, Morrison's *Paradise* moves beyond while retaining the ideals of the movement, as evidenced by the centrality of the novel of the community of women living in the Convent. Indeed, *Paradise* positions the convent women as the best hope for moving past racism and patriarchal structures which the novel presents as interrelated, and toward an alternative, non-hierarchically based form of justice that emphasizes coalition and community: coalition in the sense of joining forces to strive for specific goals, and community in the sense of a communitarian space. Moreover, the novel explores the interdependence of the coalition and community as means of reconfiguring a communal form of agency. The Convent provides a space that not only ensures temporary survival to all those who find their way there regardless of race, class, age, or past history—but also validates ordinary women and "their small stories" (p. 212) to the extent that collectively they can construct subject positions for themselves that include positions other than that of subjugation. On one level, survival entails a loving mutual, co-operative nurturing within the framework of this community; each woman is nurtured by, at the same time that she provides nurturing to, the others. Moreover, although the community appears separatist in its geographical marginality as well as its exclusively female membership, the novel presents the community of women living in the Convent at the edge of Ruby as able to negotiate a separatism that is merely temporary, that is constructive and inclusive, that reconceptualizes power as power with rather than power over, and that depends on dynamic coalition practices.

Paradise employs Morrison's familiar techniques. The story switches back and forth from the past to the present, from one character's point of view to another:

> There are gratuitous biblical allusions (like comparing the story of Ruby's founders to the story of the holy family, turned away from the inn and more gratuitous suggestions that the women at the convent are feminist martyrs, like the witches of Salem. (Deirure, *Today*, p. 3)

The remainder of *Paradise* is devoted to explaining who these men are and what brought their intended victims to the convent in the first place. We learn that the townsmen have never been able to move past their village's history.

In Morrison's last three novels the focus is on the relationship between excessive love and violence. From the opening line, "They shoot the White girl first" (p. 3), through the final paragraph, the narrative voice consistently moves the story forward with numerous flashbacks. As in a town woman's description of the sign that preceded the first visit of her friend:

> She had been upstairs, tidying the little foreclosed house, and paused to look through a bedroom window. Down below the leaf-heavy trees were immobile as a painting. July. Dry. One hundred one degrees. Still, opening the windows would freshen the room that had been empty for a year. . . . Then a mighty hand dug deep into a giant sack and threw fistfuls of petals into the air. Or so it seemed. Butterflies. A trembling highway of persimmon –

> colored wings cut across the green treetops forever – then vanished. (p. 90)

Morrison's narrative voice, which created masterful effects in both *Beloved* and *Jazz,* approaches perfection in this novel by approaching, in its unique way, the African-American experience. Morrison introduces an enormous number of characters and imagines immensely complicated relationships in creating the life of an entire town from its founding to the disastrous events that force it to face up to harsh realities.

In this novel, as in her all other novels, Morrison has beautifully described the life of an African-American Community and the women, men and children in it. She also examines the conflict between generations, the significance of race, the customs of religion and the very meaning of paradise.

In this novel there are racial differences because the society has been constructed along racial divisions. In Morrison's view, "race is the least important piece of information we have about another person. Forcing people react racially to another person is to miss the whole point of humanity" (Verdilla, p. 8). In *Paradise* Morrison wanted to talk about "the nature of racial hierarchy that it comes in all shapes and forms and in all sorts of cultures" (Verdilla, p. 8). Richard Edber in his review of Toni Morrison's *Paradise* comments,

> It's a fascinating story, wonderfully detailed by Morrison's shrewd and vivid portraits of Ruby's citizens and forebears. But the author has done more than that. Her town is the stage for a profound and provocative debate – always personified and always searching about black identity and destiny in America's past and present. (p. 7)

Conclusion

Through a comprehensive examination of Morrison's works the previous chapters explored the lives of women whose only crime is their colour, gender and poverty, and who must suffer because they are born African-American female and poor in a world where only the White, male and rich are cherished and considered human or worthy of attention. Such women throughout history and in contemporary society in life and in literature have traditionally been overlooked, undermined and stereotyped. They have existed only on the periphery of society, inhabiting marginal worlds, playing servile roles. Gloria Wade Gayles has perhaps provided the best description of the African-American woman's position in White American society. She contends that there are

> three major circles of reality in American society, which reflect degrees of power and powerlessness. There is a large circle in which White people, most of them men, experience influence and power. Far away from it there is a smaller circle, a narrow space, in which African-American people, regardless of sex, experience uncertainty, exploitation, and powerlessness. Hidden in this second is a third, a small dark enclosure in which African-American women experience pain, isolation and vulnerability. These

> are the distinguishing marks of African-American womanhood in White America. . . . African-American women are thus confined to both the narrow space of race and the dark enclosure of sex. This 'double jeopardy' has created a complex, painful, and dehumanizing reality in which they have struggled for freedom and selfhood. . . . And yet their unique position in American culture is often ignored or minimized in studies of the impact of race and sex on American values, lifestyles and economic groupings. (*No Crystal Stair,* pp. 3-4)

From her very first novel, Morrison's attempt has been to pull such women out of the anonymity of existence and place them at the nucleus, the throbbing heart, of literature. Morrison's writing is a protest against exploitation. She creates characters beyond the stereotype of the Nigger, slave, and mammy by placing them in key positions and meaningful roles. She endows them with respectability and honour by allowing them to take control of their lives, assume responsibility for themselves, and make choices that suit them best. It gives them an opportunity to become subjects in a world that has only treated them as objects so far.

Although she writes with the aim of retrieving a respectful place for African-American women in literature, Morrison never elevates or glorifies her heroines beyond believability. She does not write about infallible, morally upright, virtuous women who can do no wrong. She creates characters who resemble normal African-American people and are as prone to mistakes as the next person. Her heroines strive for visibility in a society in which blackness signifies invisibility.

Furthermore Morrison speaks of her writing as "archaeological explorations", one of her most important concerns being the rewriting of African-American history from an African-American female perspective. Until the 1940s African-American women, whether in Anglo or African-American literature, have been usually assigned stereotyped roles. Throughout the novels of slavery and reconstruction, southern White literature fashioned an image of the African-American woman intended to further extend their submission and created a dumping ground for those female functions, which a basically puritan society could not confront. Following the advice of Shirley Chisholm, who emphasized the necessity of talking truthfully and courageously about their plight as women, Morrison speaks out:

> I write for African-American women. We are not addressing the men, as some White female writers do. We are not attacking each other, as both Black and White men do. African-American women writers look at things in an unforgiving/loving way. They are writing to repossess, re-name, re-own. (Mckay, p. 46)

The racist, sexist, and classist structure of American Society categorizes its various ethnic groups, denigrates the colored as inferior and characterizes males and females as central and marginal respectively. As African-Americans are degraded as an underclass owing to their race, women are degraded to a separate caste owing to their sex. African women have been oppressed not only by racist and sexist assumptions but also by class oppression, which is equally responsible for the oppression of African-Americans in America. It is a prevalent myth in American society that the Whites are more intelligent and virtuous than African-Americans just because of being White. Moreover whiteness is considered synonymous with beauty and culture and blackness with ugliness and slavery.

Sexism gave a physical wound to African-American women. Thus, to be African-American and female is to endure the double disadvantages of racial discrimination and gender bias. African-American women suffer not only because they are Black and female, but also because they are poor. Race, sex and class therefore are not separate entities but are closely interlinked with one another. They are so organically interlinked that one must consider their interrelationship despite their ever-shifting appearance. Racism and sexism emanate from capitalism. The economic system of slavery, an early form of capitalism, is the cause of racism and sexism rather than the result of it.

So the roots of oppression are mutually interdependent. In the contemporary period, African-American novelists like Frances Harper, Jessie Fauset, Nella Larsen, Zola Neale Hurston, Ann Petry, Paule Marshall, and Alice Walker have continued to analyse the relation between race, gender and class. Significantly, Toni Morrison has explored in her novels, more than the others, women in connection to race and class.

The novels of Toni Morrison artistically document the writer's consciousness and concern for the historical situation of the exploitation of African-Americans in America, thereby showing her heightened awareness of the interconnection among racism, sexism and classism. Though we find all three elements in all her novels, the stress on them varies from novel to novel. Morrison explores the problems of race and sex before looking into class contradictions within the race. At the initial stage of her writing career, she felt that race was the important cause of oppression but very soon she realized that sexism was also another cause. Finally, she discovers that along with racism and sexism, capitalism is equally oppressive. In other words it has produced racism and sexism.

In Morrison's first novel, *The Bluest Eye*, the focus is on racial oppression. Mainly, she examines the influence that standards of beauty of the dominant culture have on the self-image of the African-American female adolescent. Morrison, at this stage of her literary career, considers racism to be the primary factor hindering the growth of African-Americans. *The Bluest Eye* attempts to reveal terrible consequences when African-Americans adopt White values directly and indirectly. Eleven-year-old Pecola is a poor, ugly, African-American girl who longs for an unattainable desire, a pair of blue eyes. She hopes that after fulfilling this desire she will be lovable and will be able to alleviate the manifold miseries of her hate-filled, quarrelsome violent family, ironically named Breedlove. Pecola becomes the victim of a chain of African-

American people, including her own mother and father who have been twisted and perverted by the false and often vicious standards of the White world. She is not only the victim of racism but also of sexism. As an African-American, she is compelled to relinquish her individual, cultural ways; as a female she is made inferior to her female attributes and remains trapped in the orbit of patriarchy. Though class analysis is minimal in this novel, Morrison is at least conscious of a limited role that economics plays in the exploitation of African-American people.

In Morrison's second novel, *Sula*, the emphasis is on gender. It is the story of an iconoclastic girl Sula Mac Peace whose non-conformity is a "living criticism of the dreadful lives of resignation other women live" (Smith, p. 166). As a budding youth, she shocks the entire society with her extreme emotional impulses and grows into a "strange, strong and independent woman." She rejects the accepted modes of behaviour and decides to "rely solely on herself" (Bischoff, p. 22). Even though the focus of this novel is on gender bias, the racial issues—the origin of the Bottom with its root in slavery and the lack of development of the Deweys—are woven into the fabric of the entire novel. The issue of class is only incidental, however, since the focus is on sexism.

Song of Solomon, Morrison's third novel, does not especially concentrate on the concept of the female, for its protagonists are men. However class, in relation to race and gender, becomes more focused in this novel than in *The Bluest Eye* and *Sula*. Morrison subordinates sex to both race and class, realizing that the exploitation of the African-American woman by the African-American man is the result of his racial and class oppression. Like Ralph Ellison's *Invisible Man*, *Song of Solomon* "combines the epic quest with bildungsroman motif and the search for the Grail of identity theme" (Samuels and Hudson, p. 53).

Like Alex Haley's *Roots*, it explains the significance of African-American consciousness and acceptance of their history in order to free themselves from racism and classism. Although Milkman's search for his individuality is the dominant thread of the novel, the major problem he has to conquer is the deadening effects of capitalism. He is unintentionally propelled on his quest for self as a result of his craving for gold. The long journey takes him back through his personal past to a racial history that had been fiercely opposed to materialism and avarice. His knowledge liberates him, and he starts to respect the destitute African-Americans around him as well as the women, Pilate and Hagar, who have continuously helped him. By the time of *Song of Solomon* Morrison becomes more conscious of the dialectical relationship between capitalism, racism, and sexism.

Morrison's increased class awareness is depicted in her ability and commitment to look into the cause and effect relationship between class, race, and gender as evidenced in her fourth novel, *Tar Baby*. Here her main focus is on the exploitative economic system. The two protagonists in *Tar Baby*, Son and Jadine, are sharply divided in their attitudes to the powerful ruling class as well as to their own traditional culture. They must struggle together in order to resolve their own class interests. Morrison's emphasis in *Tar Baby* is hence on the class struggle against capitalism. Racism and sexism, although equally oppressive, are treated as its by-products. In order to liberate themselves from these multiple problems, African-American people should fight collectively not individually. But, money-oriented Jadine and roots-bound Son do not struggle collectively. Her search for self is not successful due to her blind adoption of White values and customs and the rejection of her own African-American heritage. The more socially conscious Son is unsuccessful in educating politically the selfish capitalism-oriented Jadine. His failure to do so is in part due to his own seduction by the capitalist way of life. Their solutions to the common problem they confront are individual and not applicable to the collective realities of everyday life. Thus, *Tar Baby* projects only individual class struggle against capitalism, which is finally rendered fruitless.

After realising that capitalism is the paramount cause of African-American's oppression, Morrison proposes in her next novel, *Beloved*, a collective class struggle against capitalism. In this novel gender atrocity is not a visible problem, which exists between African men and women, but one that exists within the context of the economic relationship between master and slave. Like gender oppression, race oppression is examined as a consequence of the economic exploitation of African-Americans. *Beloved* is based on the most tyrannical period of slavery in the history of African masses. It dramatizes a haunting mixture of the past and present experiences of a runaway female slave, Sethe, tracing the heroine's search for meaning and wholeness in slavery and in liberty. Through flashbacks to past tragedies and the deeply symbolic delineation of her continued emotional and psychological suffering, the novel explores the hardships endured by Sethe and her family during Reconstruction. It is Morrison's aim to show that collectivism is the first step in eradicating the racial oppression and class exploitation of African-Americans. Morrison uses *Beloved* as a vehicle to propose solidarity as the remedy for African-American people. This message conveyed in terms of fictional art in *Beloved* is as follows:

> No longer should African people be physically intimidated by Europeans as in *The Bluest Eye*; no longer should African people indulge in the selfish individualism of *Sula;* no longer should African people ignore their duty to pass on the knowledge of their history as in *Song and Solomon;* and no longer should African people attempt to wage struggle alone and, thus, unsuccessfully as in *Tar Baby*. Solidarity, the theme of *Beloved*, is the solution for African people. (*Developing Class Consciousness*, p. 89)

After proposing collective class struggle against capitalism in *Beloved*, Morrison felt that the problem of sexism peculiar to women can be solved only through gender solidarity. Therefore she emphasizes the theme of women in *Jazz*, which adds a new dimension to the remedy for the dilemma of African-American women. Just as unity is a must for African-

American people to survive and to progress, so also African-American women, the most tortured adult sector in the African-American society, must help one another to live healthy and wholesome lives. Morrison's purpose is to make fiction do what the music does whereby she exploits the mode of jazz to describe the experience of the African-Americans during the 1920s, the Jazz Age. As jazz music is known for expressing various sentiments, uniting performer and audience, the fictional mode of jazz used in the novel establishes quick relations between the characters and the reader. The novel traces the path to understanding of Violet, a wronged wife, as she relates with other African-American women—Dorcas, Alice and Felice. Although it begins with Violet's inability to understand Dorcas, towards the close of the novel she is able to achieve this understanding through her interaction with Dorcas' aunt, Alice and her friend, Felice. Defining themselves through bonding on various levels, these African-American women seek their own identity.

Morrison's seventh novel, *Paradise*, is a story of redemption, of forgiveness and of renewal. It is set in the 1970s, in the tiny, self-sufficient all-Black town of Ruby, Oklahoma, a town that has reached a crisis of conviction. Tracing its origins to the efforts of a strong and spiritual community of ex-slaves, Ruby prides itself on its uncompromising independence from the larger world. But the vicissitudes of the sixties, from the Civil Rights Movement to the Vietnam war, the counterculture to the generational conflict, inexorably touch Ruby and disturb its self-imposed isolation. In the scrubland outside Ruby is an old Convent in which five women live, each seeking refuge to deliverance from a grim past. As the townspeople begin to lose their own convictions and succumb to the uncertainties of the times, they come to associate these unknown women with evil and to use the convent as an scapegoat for the anger and conflict that have overtaken their town. Tension between the two communities rises, culminating inevitably in an act of violence.

A careful study of the interconnection among racism,

sexism and classism in the novels of Toni Morrison shows the emergence of an evolutionary pattern. One can observe a progressive, thematic and structural evolution in her novels. She has used each novel as a framework for investigating manifold problems of and solution to African-Americans, especially African-American women's dilemmas. In each of her novels Morrison investigates some aspect of oppression afflicting African-American people. Each successive novel shows her growing understanding of the nature of that oppression. One can see the thread that runs through and connects novel after novel as one picks up where the other leaves off thematically and structurally.

From this it becomes explicit that Morrison gains knowledge progressively as she understands life, reads about it, writes about it and, what is more, thinks as she writes. As her knowledge of the dialectical way in which the laws of nature apply to society increases, she moves from a weak to a strong class analysis, always perceiving the role of race and sex in African-American women's oppression. And, as she begins to think about, write about, and experience the ongoing oppression of African-American people in racist America, she becomes aware of the fact that sexism is as much African-American women's enemy as race. Finally she realizes the fact that class is equally responsible for the oppression of African-American women.

Whereas each of her previous novels focuses on a different but connected factor in the oppression of African-American people, all are strongly related. In fact, each serves as a stepping stone that enables Morrison to move to the next level of discovery. Each character develops from the preceding one. The twelve-year-old Pecola becomes the twelve-year-old Sula, the thirty-year-old Sula becomes the thirty-one-year-old Milkman, the conscious Milkman, who flies away unburdened by the material objects of the capitalist world, becomes the Son who single-handedly tries to politically educate the people in vain. The unsuccessful Son becomes Paul D., who defies defeat, a part of the struggling collective, by returning again and again to struggle for his people.

The ambivalent endings of the first four novels and the confident endings of the last three can be used as examples to measure the author's own developing consciousness regarding both the nature of African-American women's oppression and the solution. *The Bluest Eye* ends with the demise of the protagonist, Pecola Breedlove, who becomes psychologically sick at the age of twelve years and miscarries her child. In *Sula*, the self-centered individualism of the protagonist, Sula Peace, brings death. In *Song of Solomon*, Milkman, having gained consciousness about himself and his people, flies away instead of passing on his political consciousness. In *Tar Baby*, a conscious, root-bound Son struggles unsuccessfully to politically educate the self-centred class-bound Jadine due to his own seduction by the capitalist way of life. But *Beloved* concludes on a note of unity by reiterating that collective struggle is the only way out for the sustenance of African people in America. In the same way, Jazz winds up on a note of female solidarity as the viable remedy for gender oppression. *Paradise* again deals with the same issue of gender solidarity.

Morrison's novels make clear that African-Americans in America suffer from a three-pronged oppression of race, gender and class. Each successive novel shows her growing understanding of the nature of solution to the African-American women's dilemma. In sum, an intimate look at the Morrison canon shows that there is a progressive pattern in her novels. One can see a thematic and structural unity not only in her individual novels but in her very canon as a whole. Each novel moves forward to a new concern but does not completely leave behind the previous ones. Thus, the movement is both linear and circular, "a Yeastian gyre that spins back on itself but inevitably leads upward to new ways of seeing old systems of belief" (Denise Heinze, p. 12). In this respect Morrison's novels can be considered, as Robert Stepto suggests, "an intratextural call and response, a progressive troping of her own works" ("From Behind the Veil", p. xi).

Works Cited

Banyiwa, Naane Horne. "The Scary Face of the Self: An Analysis of the character of Sula in Toni Morrison's *Sula*". *SAGE,* 2, 1. Spring (1985).

Bartelme, Elizabeth. "Rev of Paradise". *Commonweal Foundation.* Oct. 9. 1998: n. pag.

Beal, Frances. "Double Jeopardy: To be Black and Female." *The Black Women: An Anthology.* New York: Signet, 1970.

Beauvoir, Simone De. *The Second Sex.* Trans. H.M. Parshley. rpt. London: Picador Classics, 1988.

Bethel, Lorraine. "The Infinity of Conscious Pain: Zora Neale Hurston and the Black Female Literary Tradition." *But Some of Us Are Brave.* New York: The Feminist Press, 1982.

Bischoff, Joan. "The Novels of Toni Morrison: Studies in Thwarted Sensitivity". *Studies in Dark Literature,* 6, 3 (1975).

Braxton, Joanne M., and McLaughlin, Andree Nicola. *Wild Women In the Whirlwind: Afro-American Culture and the Contemporary Literature Renaissance.* London: Serpent's Tail, 1990.

Campbell, Josie P. "To Sing the Song, To Tell the Tale: A Study of Toni Morrison and Simone Schwarz-Bart". *Comparative Literature Studies,* 20, 3 (Fall 1985): 394-412.

Carby, Hazel. *Reconstructing Womanhood: The Emergence of the Afro-American woman Novelist*. New York: Oxford Press, 1987.

Chinweizu. *The West and the Rest of Us: White Predators, Black Slaves and the African Elite*. New York: Random House, 1975.

Christian, Barbara. *Black Feminist Criticism: Perspectives on Black Women Writers*. New York: Pergamon Press, 1985.

______. "Community and Nature: The Novels of Toni Morrison". *Journal of Ethnic Studies*, 7 (Winter 1980).

______. "Shadows Uplifted". *Feminist Criticism and Social Change: Sex, Class and Race in Literature and Culture*. Ed. Judith Newton and Deborah Rosenfelt. New York and London: Methuen, 1985.

______. "Trajectories of Self-Definition: Placing Contemporary, Afro-American Women's Fiction". *Conjuring: Black Women, Fiction and Literary Tradition*. Ed. Marjorie Pryse and Hortense Spillcr. Bloomington: University of Indiana, 1985.

Christian, Smith. "Toward a black feminist criticism". *Feminist Criticism and Social Change: Sex, Class and Race in Literature and Culture*. Ed. Judith Newton and Deborah Rosenfelt. New York and London: Methuen, 1985.

Coleman, James. "The Quest for Wholeness in Toni Morrison's *Tar Baby*". *BALF*, vol. 20, 1-2 (Spring/Summer, 1986).

Deirure, Donahire. "Morrison's Slice of *Paradise*". *U.S.A. Today*. 2001: n. page.

Donald, Gibson B. "The Text and Countertext in Toni Morrison's *The Bluest Eye*". *Literature and Interpretation Theory*. 1-2 (1989).

Dowling, Colette. "The Song of Toni Morrison". *New York Times Magazine*. 20 May, 1979.

Drimmer, Melvin, Ed. *Black History: A Reappraisal*. New York: Doubleday and Company, 1968.

Edward, Thomas R. "Ghost Story". *New York Review of Books.* 5 November 1987.

Farnhan and Lundberg. "Some Aspects of Woman's Psyche". *Women's Liberation and Literature.* Ed. Elaine Showalter. Harcourt: Brace Jovanovich, 1971.

Freiert, William K. "Classical Themes in Toni Morrison's *Song of Solomon*". *Helios* 10 (1983): 161-70.

Fridean, Betty. "The Sexual Solipsism of Sigmund Freud." *Women's Liberation and Literature.* Ed. Elaine Showalter. Harcourt: Brace Jovanovich, 1971.

Gates, Henry Louis and K.A. Appiah. Eds. *Toni Morrison: Critical Perspectives Past and Present.* New York: Amistard, 1993.

Gayles, Gloria Wade. *No Crystal Stair: Visions of Race and Sex in Black Women's Fiction.* New York: The Pilgrim Press, 1984.

Gillespie, Dinae and Missy Dehn Kubitschek. "Women Centred Psychology in *Sula*". *Toni Morrison: Critical Perspectives Past and Present.* Eds. Gates, Henry Louis and K.A. Appiah. New York: Amistard, 1993.

Harris, Trudier. *Fiction and Folklore: The Novels of Toni Morrison.* Knoxville: Univ. of Tennessee Press, 1991.

______. "Reconnecting Fragments: Afro-American Folk Tradition in *The Bluest Eye*". *Critical Essays on Toni Morrison.* Ed. Nellie Y. Mckay. Boston: Hall, 1988.

Harvard, Maureen, and John Irving. *A Study of Tar Baby.* New York: B.R. Gruner Publishing, 1993.

Heinze, Denise. *The Dilemma of "Double-Consciousness" in Toni Morrison's Novels.* Athens and London: The Univ. of Georgia Press, 1993.

Helen, Mary Washington. Ed. *Black Eyed Susan: Classic Stories by and about Black Women.* New York: Anchor Press, 1975.

Hernoton, Calvin. *Sex and Racism in America.* New York:

Grove Weidn Field, 1965 rpt. First Evergreen edition, 1998.

Jones, Jacqueline. *Labour of Love Labour of Sorrow: Black Women, Work and the Family, from Slavery to the Present.* New York: Vintage, 1985.

Kakutani, Michiko. "Paradise: Worthy Women, Unredeemable Men." Rev. of *Paradise* by Toni Morrison *Books of the Times.* January 6 (1988): n. page.

Katz, Maude White. "The Negro Woman and the Law". *Freedomways* V. 2, (1994).

Klotman, Phillis R. "Toni Morrison - 1931". *Contemporary Literary Criticism.* V. 22, N. 2 (1982).

Kovel, Joel. *White Racism: A Psychohistory.* New York: Columbia Univ. Press, 1984.

Lavon, Maxine Montgomery. "A Pilgrimage to the Origins: The Apocalypse as Structure and Theme in Toni Morrison's *Sula*". *BALF.* V. 23.1 (Spring 1989).

Leclair, Thomas. "The Language Must Not Sweet: A Conversation with Toni Morrison". An Interview with Toni Morrison. *The New Republic,* 21 Mar. 1981.

Leonard, John. "Jazz". *The Nation.* 25 May (1992).

Lowenberg, Bert J. and Ruth Bogin. Eds. *Black Women in Nineteenth Century American Life.* University Park: Pennsylvania State Univ. Press, 1976.

Mbalia, Doreatha Drummond. *Toni Morrison's Developing Class Consciousness.* Selingrove: Subsquehana Univ. Press, 1992.

______. "Women who Run with Wild: The Need for Sisterhood in *Jazz*". *MFS,* V. 39, 3 and 4 (Fall/Winter, 1993).

Mckay, Nellie, Y. Ed. *Critical Essays on Toni Morrison.* Boston: Hall, 1988.

Michele, Wallace. "A Black Feminist's Search for Sisterhood". *The Village Voice.* 28 July 1975. pp. 6-7, rpt. pp. 5-12.

Morrison, Toni. "Behind the Making of *The Black Book*". *Black World*. V. 23, 1974.

Murthy, Yamini K. "Gender Solidarity and Discovery of Self in Morrison's *Tar Baby* and *Jazz*". *IJAS*, V. 23, 2 (Summer, 1993).

Mwanamke, Mwananchi. "The Nationalist Woman". Mumininas of Committee for Unified Newark. Newark, N.J., C. 1971, pp. 4-5.

Parker, Bettye. "Complexity: Toni Morrison's Women An Interview Essay". *Sturdy Black Bridges: Vision of Black Women in Literature*. Ed. Roseann P. Bell, Betty J. Parker, and Beverly Guy-Sheftall. New York: Anchor Press, 1979.

Parmar, Sumita. "Establishing Visibility: Contemporary Fiction by Afro-American Women Writers". *Feminism and Recent Fiction in English*. Ed. Sushila Singh, New Delhi: Prestige, 1991.

Plakkoottam, Alphy J. "The Dynamics of Man-Woman Relationships in Toni Morrison's *Song of Solomon* and Mariama Ba's *So Long a Letter*". *IJAS*, V. 233 (Summer 1993).

Puri, Usha. "Toni Morrison: Redefining Feminine Space in *Beloved*". *IJAS*, 1993.

______. *Towards a New Womanhood*. Jaipur: Printwell Publishers, 1989.

Ranveer, Kashinath. *Black Feminist Consciousness: A Study of Black Female Authors*. Delhi: Rupa Pub., 1995.

Ray, Arunima. "The Quest for 'Home' and 'Wholeness' in *Sula* and *Meridian*: Afro-American Identity in Toni Morrison and Alice Walker". *IJAS*, V. 23, 2 Summer, 1993.

Richard, Edber in *The Los Angels Times*. Sunday Book Review. n. d. page.

Rodney, Walter. *How Europe Underdeveloped Africa*. Dar es Salaam: Tanzania Publishing House, 1972.

Ryan, Judylyns. "Contested vision/Double Vision in *Tar Baby*". *MFS*, V. 39, 3-4 (Fall/Winter 1993).

Samuels, Wilfred D. and Clenora Hudson-weems. Eds. *Toni Morrison* Boston: Twayne Press, 1990.

Shockley, Evelyn E. Rev. of *Paradise. African American Review.* Winter. 1999: n. page.

Showalter, Elaine Ed. *Women's Liberation and Literature.* Harcourt: Brace Jovanovich, 1971.

Smith, Barbara. "Toward a Black Feminist Criticism." *All the Women are White, All the Blacks are Men but Some of Us are Brave: Black Women Studies.* Ed. Gloira T. Hull, Patricia Bellscott and Barbara Smith. New York: Feminist Press, 1982.

Smith, Valerie. *Self Discovery and Authority in Afro-American Narrative.* Cambridge: Harvard Univ. Press, 1987.

Stepto, Robert. *From Behind the Veil: A Study of Afro-American Narrative.* Urbana: University of Illinois Press, 1979.

_____. "Intimate Things in Place: A Conversation with Toni Morrison". An Interview with Toni Morrison. Chants of Saints Urbana: Univ. of Illinois Press, 1979.

Strouse, Jean. "Toni Morrison: Black Magic". *Newsweek,* 30 March (1981).

Swain, S.P. "Roots and Shadows - A Feminist Study". *Feminist English Literature.* Ed. Manmohan Bhatnagar. Delhi: Atlantic Publisher, 1999.

______. "The Novels of Toni Morrison: A Feminist Study". *Feminist English Literature.* Ed. Manmohan Bhatnagar. Delhi: Atlantic Publisher, 1999.

Turner, Darwin T. "Theme Characterization and Style in the Works of Toni Morrison". *Black Women Writers: Critical Evaluation.* (1950 - 1980). Ed. Meri Evans. New York: Anchor Book, 1984.

Verdella, A. J. *Paradise Found: A Talk with Toni Morrison Abut*

Her New Novel, Paradise. Commonweal Foundation, February 1998: n. page.

Williams, Eric. *Capitalism and Slavery*. New York: G.P. Putnam's, 1944.

Young, Reggie. Review of *Paradise*, 18 Mar. 1998: n. page.

Selected Bibliography

Primary Sources

Fiction

Beloved. London: Vintage, 1987.

The Bluest Eye. London: Picador, 1970.

Jazz. London: Picador, 1992.

Paradise. London: Chatto and Windus, 1997.

Song of Solomon. Britain: Granada, 1977.

Sula. London: Picador. 1973.

Tar Baby. London: Vintage, 1981.

Miscellaneous

"Recitatif" [short story], *Confirmation: An Anthology of African American Women*. Ed. Amiri Baraka and Amina Baraka. New York: Quill. 1983. 243-61.

Dreaming Emmett [play]. Performed 4 January 1986 by the Capital Repertory Theater in Albany, New York.

Edited Collections

The Black Boo. Comp. Middleton Harris, et al. [Ed Toni Morrison]. NY: Random House, 1974.

Race-ing Justice, En-Gendering Power. Essays on Anita Hill,

Clarence Thomas, and the Construction of Social Reality. Ed. Toni Morrison. New York: Pantheon.

Essays

"To Be a Black Woman". *New York Times Magazine*. 28 March 1971, 8.

"What the Black Woman Thinks About Women's Lib". *New York Times Magazine*. 22 August 1971, 14-15, 63-66.

"Behind the Making of the Black Book". *Black World*. February 1974, 86.90.

"Rediscovering Black History". *New York Times Magazine*. 11 August 1974, 14, 16, 18, 20, 22, 24.

"Reading". *Mademoiselle*. May 1975, 14.

"A Slow Walk of Trees (as Grandmother Would Say) Hopeless (as Grandfather Would Say". *New York Times Magazine*. 4 July 1976, 104-5, 150-64.

"I Will Always Be a Writer". *Essence*. December 1976, 54-56, 90.

Foreword. *The Harlem Book of the Dead* by James Van Der Zee. Owen Dodson, and Camille Billops. Dobbs Ferry, NY: Morgan and Morgan, 1978, n.p.

"The Lesson of Cinderella's Stepsisters." Ms., September 1979, 41-42.

"City Limits, Village Values: Concepts of the Neighborhood in Black Fiction." *Literature and the Urban Experience*. Ed. Michael C. Jaye and Ann Chalmers Watts. New Brunswick: Rutgers University Press, 1981, 35-43.

"Writers Together: Address given at the American Writers' Congress", 9 October 1981. *Nation*. 24 October 1981, 396 ff.

"Memory, Creation, and Writing". *Thought*. December 1984, 385-90.

"Rootedness: The Ancestor as Foundation." *Black Women Writers (1950-1980): A Critical Evaluation*. Ed. Mari Evans. Garden City, NY: Anchor-Doubleday, 1984, 339-45.

"A Knowing So Deep". *Essence*. May 1985, 230.

"Faulkner and Women". *Faulkner and Yoknapatawpha*. Ed. Doreen Fowler and Ann J. Abadie. Jackson: University of Mississippi Press, 1986, 295-302.

"The Site of Memory". *Inventing the Truth: The Art and Craft of Memoir*. Ed. William Zinnser. Boston: Houghton Mifflin, 1987, 103-24.

"On Behalf of Henry Dumas." *Black American Literature Forum*. 22 (1988), 310-12.

"Unspeakable Things Unspoken: The African American Presence in American Literature". *Michigan Quarterly Review*. 28 (1989), 1-34.

Playing in the Dark: Whiteness and the Literary Imagination. Cambridge: Harvard University Press, 1992.

"Introduction: Friday on the Potomac". *Race-ing Justice, Engendering Power*. vii-xxx.

"Nobel Lecture 1993". *World Literature Today*. 68 (1994), 5-8.

Interviews

Conversations with Toni Morrison. Ed. Danille Taylor-Guthrie. Jackson: UP of Mississippi, 1994.

Toni Morrison: Profile of a Writer. Videotape. Prod. and Dir. Alan Benson. Ed. Melvyn Bragg. LWT/RM arts, 1987. 52 min.

Toni Morrison. Videotape. Part 3 of *In Black and White. Six Profiles of African American Writers*. Dir. Matteo Bellinelli—. Prod. RTSI-Swiss Television. California Newsreel. 1992. 27 min.

Biographies

Folsom, Tonya. "Toni Morrison Bibliography: 1990-93". *Toni Morrison Society Newsletter*. 1.1 (1984), 8-11.

Middleton, David L. *Toni Morrison: An Annotated Bibliography.* New York: Garland, 1987.

Books on Toni Morrison

Bijork, Patrick Bryce. *The Novels of Toni Morrison: The Search for Self and Place within the Community.* New York: Peter Lang, 1992.

Bloom, Harold. Ed. *Toni Morrison.* New York: Chelsea House, 1990.

Gates, Henry Louis, Jr. and K.A. Appiah. Eds. *Toni Morrison: Critical Perspectives Past and Present* Amistad Literary Series. New York: Amistad, 1993.

Harris, Trudier. *Fiction and Folklore: The Novels of Toni Morrison.* Knoxville: University of Tennessee Press, 1991.

Heinze, Denise. *The Dilemma of "Double-Consciousness": Toni Morrison's Novels.* Athens: U of Georgia P, 1993.

Holloway, Karla F.C. and Stephanie A. Demetrakopoulos. *New Dimensions of Spirituality: A Biracial and Bicultural Reading of the Novels of Toni Morrison.* New York: Greenwood, 1987.

Jones, Bessie W. and Audrey L. Vinson. *The World of Toni Morrison: Explorations in Literary Criticism.* Dubuque, IA: Kendall/Hunt, 1985.

Mbalia, Doreatha Drummond. *Toni Morrison's Developing Class Consciousness.* Selingrove: Susquehanna UP, 1991.

Mckay, Nellie Y., ed. *Critical Essays on Toni Morrison.* Boston: Hall, 1988.

Samuels, Wilfred D., and Clenora Hudson-Weems. *Toni Morrison.* Boston: Twayne, 1990.

Books that Include Toni Morrison

Butler-Evans, Elliott. *Race, Gender, and Desiree: Narrative Strategies in the Fiction of Toni Cade Bambara, Toni Morrison, and Alice Walker.* Philadelphia: Temple University Press, 1989.

Christian. Barbara T. *Black Feminist Criticism.* New York: Pergamon, 1985, 47-80.

______. *Black Women Novelists: The Development of Tradition* 1892-1976. Westport. CT: Greenwood, 1980. 137-79, 239-52.

de Weever, Jacqueline. *Mythmaking and Metaphor in Black Women's Fiction.* New York: St. Martin's, 1992.

Kubitschek. Missy Dehn. *Claiming the Heritage: African American Women Novelists and History.* Jackson: University Press of Mississippi, 1991.

Mobley, Marilyn Sanders. *Folk Roots and Mythic Wings in Sarah Orne Jewett and Toni Morrison: The Cultural Function of Narrative.* Baton Rouge: Louisiana State University Press, 1991.

Smith, Valerie. *Self-Discovery and Authority in Afro-American Narrative.* Cambridge: Harvard UP, 1987. 122-53.

Relevant General Articles

Bakerman, Jane S. "Failures of Love: Female Initiation in the Novels of Toni Morrison". *American Literature.* 52 (1981), 541-63.

Bischoff, Joan. "The Novels of Toni Morrison: Studies in Thwarted Sensitivity". *Studies in Black Literature,* 6 (1975), 21-23.

Beyerman, Keith. "Remembering History in Contemporary Black Literature and Criticism". *American Literary History.* 3 (1991), 809-16.

Davis, Cynthia A. "Self, Society, and Myth in Toni Morrison's Fiction." *Contemporary Literature.* 23 (1982), 323-42.

Denard, Carolyn C. "Toni Morrison". *Modern American Women Writers.* Ed. Elaine Showalter. New York: Schribher's 1991. 317-38.

de Weever, Jacqualine. "The Inverted World of Toni Morrison's *The Bluest Eye and Sula*". *CLA Journal.* 22 (1979), 402-14.

Holloway, Karla F.C. and Stephanie Demetrakopoulos. "Remembering Our Foremothers: Older Black Women, Politics of Age, Politics of Survival as Embodied in the Novels of Toni Morrison". *Women and Politics.* 6 (1986), 13-34.

House, Elizabeth B. "The 'Sweet Life' in Morrison's Fiction". *American Literature.* 56 (1984), 181-202.

Lee, Dorothy H. "The Quest of Self: Triumph and Failure in the Works of Toni Morrison". *Black Women Writers (1950 - 1980): A Critical Evaluation.* Ed. Mari Evans. Garden City, NY: Anchor-Doubleday, 1984. 346-60.

Mobley, Marliyn S. "The Mellow Moods and Difficult Truths of Toni Morrison". *Southern Review.* 29 (1993), 614-28.

Rainwater, Catherine. "Worthy Messengers: Narrative Voices in Toni Morrison's Novels." *Texas Studies in Literature and Language.* 33 (1991), 96-113.

Turner, Darwin T. "Theme, Characterization, and Style in the Works of Toni Morrison." *Black Women Writers (1950-1980): A Critical Evaluation.* Ed. Mari Evans. Garden City, NY: Anchor-Doubleday, 1984. 361-69.

Wade-Gayles, Gloria. "The Truths of Our Mother's Lives: Mother-Daughter Relationships in Black Women's Fiction." *SAGE.* 1, 2 (1984), 8–12.

Willis, Susan. "I Shop Therefore I Am: Is There a Place for Afro-American Culture in Commodity Culture?" *Changing Our Own Words: Essays on Criticism, Theory, and Writing by Black Women.* Ed. Cheryl Wall. New Brunswick, NJ: Rutgers UP, 1989. 173-95.

Articles on Toni Morrison's Novels

(i) *The Bluest Eye*

Baum, Rosalie Murphy. "Alcoholism and Family Abuse in *Maggie* and *The Bluest Eye*". *Mosaic.* 19, 3 (1986), 91-105.

Bennett, Paula. "The Mother's Part: Insect and Maternal

Deprivation in Woolf and Morrison." *Narrating Mothers: Theorizing Maternal Subjectivities.* Ed. Brenda O Daly and Maureen T. Reddy. Knox-Villie: U of Tennessee P, 1991. 125-38.

Bishop, John. "Morrison's *The Bluest Eye." Explicator.* 51 (1993), 152-55.

Gibson, Donald B. "Text and Countertext in Toni Morrison's *The Bluest Eye*". *LIT.* 1 (1989), 19-32.

Klotman, Phyllis R. "Dick-and-Jane and Shirley Temple Sensibility in *The Bluest Eye*". *Black American Literature Forum.* 13 (1979), 123-25.

Ogunyemi, Chikwenye Okonjo. "Order and Disorder in Toni Morrison's *The Bluest Eye*". *Critique.* 19 (1977), 112-20.

Pettis, Joyce. "Difficult Survival: Mothers and Daughters in *The Bluest Eye*". *SAGE.* 4, 2, (1987), 26-29.

Rosenberg, Ruth. "Seeds in Hard Ground: Black Girlhood in *The Bluest Eye*". *Black American Literature Forum.* 21 (1987), 435-45.

Royster, Philip M. "*The Bluest Eye*". *First World.* 1, 4 (1977), 34-44.

Wong, Shelley. "Transgression and Poesis in *The Bluest Eye*". *Callaloo.* 13 (1990), 471-81.

(ii) *Sula*

Banyiwa-Horne, Naana. "The Scary Face of the Self: An Analysis of the Character of Sula in Toni Morrison's *Sula*". *SAGE.* 2, 1 (1985), 28-31.

Coleman, Alisha R. "One and One Make One: A Metacritical and Psychoanalytical Reading of Friendship in Toni Morrison's *Sula*". *CLA Journal.* 37, 8 (1993), 145-55.

Hunt, Patricia. "War and Peace: Transfigured Categories and the Politics of *Sula*". *African American Review.* 27 (1993), 443-59.

McDowell, Deborah E. "Boundaries: Or Distant Relations

and Close Kin". *Afro-American Literary Study in the 1990s.* Ed. Houston A. Baker Jr., and Patricia Redmond. Chicago: University of Chicago Press, 1989, 51-70.

Middleton, Victoria. "*Sula*: An Experimental Life". *CLA Journal.* 28 (1985), 367-81.

Ogunyemi, Chikwenye Okonjo. "*Sula*: 'A Nigger Joke'". *Black American Literature Forum.* 13 (1979), 130-33.

Smith, Barbara. "Toward a Black Feminist Criticism". *In the Memory and Spirit of Frances. Zora, and Lorraine: Essays and Interviews on Black Women and Writing.* Ed. Juliette Bowels. Washington, DC: Institute for the Arts and Humanities, *Howard U, 1979, 32-40.*

Spillers, Hortense J. "A Hateful Passion, A Lost Love." *Feminist Studies.* 9 (1983), 293-323.

Wessling, Joseph H. "Narcissism in Toni Morrison's *Sula*". *CLA Journal.* 31 (1988), 281-98.

(iii) *Song of Solomon*

Awkward, Michael. "'Unruly and Let Loose': Myth, Ideology, and Gender in *Song of Solomon*". *Callaloo.* 13 (1990), 482-98.

Blake, Susan L. "Folklore and Community in Song of Solomon". *MELUS.* 7, 3 (1980), 77-82.

Bruck, Peter. "Returning to One's Roots: The Motif of Searching and Flying in Toni Morrison's *Song of Solomon*". *The Afro-American Novel since 1960.* Ed. Peter Bruck and Wolfgang Karrer. Amsterdam: Gruner, 1982, 289-305.

Coleman, James A. "Beyond the Reach of Love and Caring: Black Life in Toni Morrison's *Song of Solomon*". *Obsidian.* II, 1,3 (1986), 151-61.

Cooper, Barhara E. "Milkman's Search for Family in Toni Morrison's *Song of Solomon*". *CLA Journal.* 33 (1989), 145-56.

Cowart, David. "Faulkner and Joyce in Toni Morrison's *Song of Solomon*". *American Literature.* 62 (1990), 87-100.

Demetrakopoulos, Stephanie. "The Nursing Mother and Feminine Metaphysics: An Essay on Embodiment". *Soundings.* 65 (1982), 430-43.

Freiert, William K. "Classical Themes in Toni Morrison's *Song of Solomon*". *Helios.* 10 (1983), 161-70.

Rabinowitz, Paula. "Naming, Magic, and Documentary: The Subversion of Narrative in *Song of Solomon, Ceremony,* and *China Men*". *Feminist Re-Visions: What Has Been and Might Be.* Ed. Vivian Patraka and Louise A. Tilly. Ann Arbor: University of Michigan Press, 1983. 26-42.

Reed, Harry. "Toni Morrison's *Song of Solomon,* and Black Cultural Nationalism". *Centennial Review.* 32 (1988), 50-64.

Samuels, Wilfred D. "Liminality and the Search for Self in Toni Morrison's *Song of Solomon*". *Minority Voices.* 5 (1981), 59-68.

Spallino, Chiara. "*Song of Solomon.* An Adventure in Structure". *Callaloo.* 8 (1985), 510-24.

Wegs, Joyce. "Toni Morrison's *Song of Solomon.* A Blues Song". *Essays in Literature.* 9 (1982), 211-23.

(iv) *Tar Baby*

Coleman, James. "The Quest for Wholeness in Toni Morrison's *Tar Baby*". *Black American Literature Forum.* 20 (1986), 67-73.

Fishman, Charles. "Naming Names: Three Recent Novels by Women Writers". *Names.* 32 (1984), 33-44.

Hawthorn, Evelyn. "On Gaining the Double-Vision: *Tar Baby* as Diasporean Novel". *Black American Literature Forum.* 22 (1988), 97-107.

Traylor, Eleanor W. "The Fabulous World of Toni Morrison: *Tar Baby.*" *Confirmation: An Anthology of African Women.* Ed. Amiri Baraka and Amina Baraka. New York: Quill, 1983. 333-52.

Walther, Malin LaVon. "Toni Morrison's *Tar Baby*: Re-Figuring the Colonizer's Aesthetics". *Cross-Cultural Performance: Differences in Women's Re-Visions of Shakespeare*. Ed. Marianne Novy. Urbana: University of Illinois Press, 1993. 137-49.

(v) *Beloved*

Atlas, Marilyn Judith. "Toni Morrison's "*Beloved* and the Reviewers". *Midwestern Miscellany*. 18 (1990), 46-57.

Bell, Bernard W. "*Beloved*: A Womanist Neo-Slave Narrative: or Multivocal Remembrances of Things Past". *African American Review*. 26 (1992), 7-15.

Christian, Barbara. "'Somebody Forgot to Tell Somebody Something': African-American Women's Historical Novels." *Wild Women in the Whirlwind*. Ed. Joanne M. Braxton and Andre Nicola McLaughlin. New Brunswick: Rutgers Press; 1990, 326-41.

Davis, Christina. "*Beloved*: A Question of Identity". *Presence Africaine*. 145 (1988), 141-50.

Demetrakopoulos, Stephanie A. "Maternal Bonds as Devourers of Women's Individuation in Toni Morrison's *Beloved*". *African American Review*. 26 (1992), 51-59.

Holloway, Karla F.C. "*Beloved* A Spiritual". *Callaloo*. 13 (1990), 516-25.

House, Elizabeth B. "Toni Morrison's Ghost: the Beloved Who Is Not Beloved". *Studies in American Fiction*. 18 (1990), 17-26.

Mathieson, Barbara Offutt. "Memory and Mother Love in Morrison's *Beloved*". *American Image*. 47, 1 (1990), 1-21.

Rigney, Barbara Hill. "'A Story to Pass on': Ghosts and the Significance of History in Toni Morrison's *Beloved*". *Haunting the House of Fiction: Feminist Perspectives on Ghost Stories by American Women*. Ed. Lynette Carpenter and Wendy K. Kolmar. Knoxville: University of Tennessee Press, 1991, 229-35.

Travis, Molly Abel. "Speaking from the Silence of the Slave Narrative: *Beloved* and African-American Women's History". *Texas Review.* 13 (1992), 69-81.

Turner, Margaret E. "Power, Language and Gender: Writing History in *Beloved* and Obasan". *Mosaic.* 25, 4 (1992), 81-97.

Wyatt, Jean. "Giving Body to the World: The Maternal Symbolic in Toni Morrison's *Beloved*". *PMLA.* 108 (1993), 474-88.

(vi) *Jazz*

Bawer, Bruce. "All that Jazz." *New Criterion.* 10, 9 (1992), 10-17.

Leonard, John. "*Jazz* (1992)". *The Nation.* 25 May, 1992.

Mbalia, Doreatha Drummond. "Women Who Run with Wild: The Need for Sisterhoods in *Jazz*". *Modern Fiction Studies.* 39, 384 (Fall/Winter 1993), 623.

Puri, Usha. "The Morrison Music: Narrative Style in *Jazz*". *Indian Journal of American Studies.* 23, 2 (Summer 1993), 59.

(vii) *Paradise*

Bartelme, Elizabeth. "Rev of *Paradise*". *Commonweal Foundation.* Oct 9. 1998: n. page.

Deirure, Donahire. "Morrison's slice of Paradise". *U.S.A. Today.* 2001: n. page.

Edber, Richard. "Rev of *Paradise*". *Loss Angels Times.* Sunday Book Review: n. d. page.

Kakutani, Michiko. "Paradise: Worthy women, unredeemable Men". Rev of *Paradise* by Toni Morrison. *Books of the Times,* 6 January 1998.

Scockley, Evelyn E. "Rev. of *Paradise*", *African American Review.* Winter. 1999: n. page.

Verdilla, A. J. "Paradise Found: A Talk with Toni Morrison About Her New Novel, *Paradise*". *Commonweal Foundation.* New York. February 1998: n. pag.

Young, Reggie. "Rev. of *Paradise*". *The Christian Century Foundation.* 18 March 1998: n. page.

Index